CHARLES DARWIN
IN SHREWSBURY

THE MAKING OF A MARVELLOUS MIND

JON FRASER KING

AMBERLEY

A chalk drawing of the seven-year-old Darwin in 1816, with a potted plant.

'I was born a naturalist'
Autobiography, *Charles Darwin*,
1876

'The Child is the Father of the Man'
The Rainbow, *Wordsworth*, 1802

First published 2023

Amberley Publishing, The Hill, Stroud
Gloucestershire GL5 4EP

www.amberley-books.com

British Library Cataloguing in Publication Data.
A catalogue record for this book is available from the British Library.

ISBN 978 1 3981 1604 7 (print)
ISBN 978 1 3981 1605 4 (ebook)

Typesetting by SJmagic DESIGN SERVICES, India.
Printed in Great Britain.

Contents

Acknowledgements

I began this project during the first Covid lockdown of 2020 but the research and background investigations began over twenty years earlier during my time as a broadcaster. My Darwin journey began with an interview with local historian Henri Quinn. Henri was a Darwin enthusiast who expressed his dismay that Shrewsbury didn't make enough of its famous son. Henri was my inspiration when I founded the Shrewsbury Darwin Festival in 2003. Some months earlier, I had interviewed Randal Keynes, a Darwin descendant who was in town to give a lecture. As we stood on the terrace at the rear of Darwin's childhood home, I floated the idea of the festival. Randal kindly gave his approval and over the next few years and during the bicentennial celebrations, he continued to give his support for which I will always be grateful. My research was helped greatly by a kind gift from the town's then Tourism Officer, Alison Patrick, who gave me a copy of a double autobiography of Charles Darwin and Thomas Huxley. The book was a revelation and I am indebted to Alison for providing me with a new perspective and one that has guided the narrative of this book. I would like to thank Emma Micklewright at Shrewsbury School for casting an expert eye over the chapter on Darwin's Big Idea and Naomi Nicholas for allowing me access to the school's collection of Darwin letters and memorabilia. To my big sister, Susan, for being a critical friend of the early drafts. Thanks to my editor Nick Grant and the team at Amberley for their support. Last and by no means least, to my wife for her patience and unstinting belief that I'd get into print someday. This is for you.

The material for this book has been compiled from personal research, archive material, and various websites and has been used in good faith. Historic images have been found from sources in the public domain and are, to the best of the author's knowledge, out of copyright. Where required, permission has been sought from the owners of properties photographed by the author who would like to thank English Heritage, The Ironbridge Gorge Museum Trust, Shrewsbury Library, Shrewsbury School and The Shropshire Wildlife Trust. Every attempt has been made to seek permission for copyright material used in this book. However, if we have inadvertently used copyright material without permission/acknowledgement we apologise and will make the necessary correction at the first opportunity.

Introduction

Picture if you will a mediocre school student, born into privilege and unable to apply himself to his studies. He is obsessed with the country sports of fishing and shooting and is a constant source of frustration and disappointment to his father. If he impresses little in his school years, he does no better at university where he takes an instant dislike to the subjects his father has chosen for him and instead takes every opportunity to stubbornly follow his own interests. Annoyingly, he is well aware that he can fritter away his time in academia because the wealth he will soon be gifted will allow him to see out his days in carefree comfort.

But our hero is not destined for the ranks of the idle rich. An accident of birth and an intellectual legacy from his grandfathers ensure that he will not be content to live in a state of blissful ignorance but embrace a family culture of curiosity. It will become an insatiable hunger that stays with him throughout his life. Financial stability simply provides the conditions by which his great ideas are conceived, notions that can be considered with the luxury of time.

I should declare from the outset that this is not the story of a bearded, elderly academic; our protagonist is in the prime of his youth with boundless energy, intrigued by the world he sees around him. His great works are years ahead but in front of him now is a period of self-reflection and personal development as a restless spirit is transformed into a towering, scientific figure. This is the story of Shrewsbury's Darwin.

The Three Pillars

We are all to a lesser or greater extent the sum of our experiences and significant amongst those are the ones we encounter in our formative years. The moments that make us who we are can be as brief as a cutting remark that cause us to question our self-image or as profound as the influence of a teacher who inspires us and sets us on a particular course. This book concerns itself with the moments that made a remarkable mind, that of Charles Darwin, the author of *On the Origin of Species*.

Darwin himself remembers many early incidents in his autobiographical writings, some of which feature in this book, but to gain an insight into the incredible journey that he undertook into adulthood it may be helpful to distil those experiences. I suggest that it is possible to account for the direction of Darwin's thinking by

The Darwin Gate, unveiled in 2003, designed by Renn & Thacker.

focussing on three important factors or pillars as I describe them. These pillars are at the core of Darwin's experiences in Shrewsbury and helped to mould the ideal candidate for Naturalist on HMS *Beagle*. As the story of Darwin's early life unfolds through the pages of this book, the pillars will be revealed.

In Shrewsbury, at the top of a street called Mardol, stands a piece of public art called the Darwin Gate, designed by Renn & Thacker and unveiled in 2004. The piece consists of three metal posts, each one sheathed by thick glass rings. At the top of each post are finials that echo ecclesiastical arches similar to those in St Mary's Church nearby. The headpieces do not meet but walk a few steps down the street and the three posts appear to form one complete structure. It is a clever optical illusion and one to which many visitors to the town are oblivious.

During my research, it occurred to me that the Darwin Gate could become a visual metaphor to symbolise the key influences that helped Shrewsbury to mould a world-class naturalist, the coming together of disparate ideas into one clear proposition, The Three Pillars. Each year, on Darwin's birthday, the structure is the penultimate stage of a guided walk that tells the story of his early life in Shrewsbury.

A clever illusion as the three key influences on Darwin's development appear to come together in one great idea.

1

Shrewsbury – The Jewel on the Severn

Charles Darwin was born in the English town of Shrewsbury on 12 February 1809 and continued to be a resident until his departure on 16 December 1837 at the age of twenty-eight. By that time he had attended two universities and undertaken a five-year voyage on HMS *Beagle*. His account of that voyage was later published and became an instant hit but the notions that filled his head as a consequence of those experiences were to lead to something much more significant. After years of reflection and, as we will learn later, a bolt from the blue, Darwin published his theory on the origin of species based partly on his observations made during the voyage.

Little has changed in Shrewsbury since Darwin's time. The streets would be familiar to him today and walking through the narrow alleyways, or shuts and passages as they are locally known, past timber-framed shops and Georgian terraces, one could easily imagine the young schoolboy hurrying to class from his family home across the River Severn.

Shrewsbury boasts many buildings and sites that were the scene of pivotal moments in his early life. As a consequence, the location of Darwin's birth has far greater significance than say Stratford has in the story of Shakespeare. There is a long tradition of placing plaques on houses or opening city museums to mark the birthplace of the famous son or daughter of a town but in Shrewsbury, Darwin's story plays out across the town itself and is written on the walls and cobbled streets, if you know where to look.

The fact that Darwin was able to exploit the opportunity of a lifetime is in no small way due to the manner and location of his upbringing. In an autobiographical fragment written in 1838, Darwin wrote 'I was born a naturalist'. He recalls that 'the passion for collecting, which leads a man to be a systematic naturalist … was very strong in me, and was clearly innate'.

Darwin seems to suggest that the notion of being a naturalist was hard-wired into him at birth; indeed he went further, writing later that 'I am inclined to agree with Francis Galton in believing that education & environment produce only a small effect on the mind of anyone, & that most of our qualities are innate.' But, as we will learn through the course of this book, it was a combination of nature and nurture that conspired to turn a young, enquiring mind into a towering figure in the history of science.

Shrewsbury is the county town of Shropshire situated in an area of England known as The Marches. To the east, the county borders the conurbation of the

Grope Lane.

West Midlands, and to the west lies Wales. The county is largely unspoiled and boasts a range of habitats from the meres and mosses of the north to the rolling hills of South Shropshire, the 'blue remembered hills' in the poet A. E. Houseman's *A Shropshire Lad*.

Today, Shropshire offers a warm welcome to visitors seeking a rural retreat but in earlier times, not all visitors were as welcome. The occupying forces of the Roman army built the town of Viroconium close to the village of Wroxeter, a little way downstream of Shrewsbury, to protect their interests in the area. In its glory years, Viroconium was the fourth largest Roman settlement in Britain. After the Roman occupation, the seat of power shifted to Shrewsbury, which became the capital of the Kingdom of Powys. Because of this, the ruins of Viroconium were not built on after the Romans left. The baths complex has been excavated and remains uncovered but the larger part lies hidden, at least a foot beneath the ground, a vast network of streets and buildings extending to around 192 acres.

The fact that these ancient remains had to be excavated to be observed was a quandary to which Darwin had given a great deal of thought. Why do we need to dig to find ancient monuments? How do they come to be underground? After years

The ruins of the Roman city of Viroconium at Wroxeter with the Wrekin Hill in the distance. (Courtesy of English Heritage)

of study, Darwin unearthed the culprit. The architect and engineer, he deduced, was the humble earthworm. In his final book published in 1881, Darwin observed how worms, moving through the earth, aerate the ground and deposit new soil on the surface in the form of worm castes. Over the years, unless swept aside, the deposits accumulate on the surface and the ancient remains slowly settle beneath them. Darwin was able to prove this in an example that demonstrates how patient a scientist he was. He spread chalk and cinders in patches on the ground in his back garden and twenty-seven years later, dug down to find them. They were 7 inches below the surface. Wroxeter Roman City, as it is now known, is managed by English Heritage and visitors to the site can see the extent to which this action has occurred. At the foot of a ditch across the road from the site entrance, the bases of a row of stone columns are visible, some distance below ground level.

Some six centuries after the Romans left, William the Conqueror's victory at Hastings saw a new era of occupation for England. Keen to secure his newly gained territory from Welsh incursions, William sent his most trusted knight, Roger de Montgomery, to guard this corner of the kingdom and ensure there were no threats to the new order. Viroconium had long since fallen into ruin

The bases of columns now below ground level. To the right is a recreation of a Roman villa built by modern craftsmen in 2011. (Courtesy of English Heritage)

and the Normans saw little sense in rebuilding it. Further upstream, Shrewsbury offered a far better strategic position. Shrewsbury town centre is built on a mound of earth squeezed into a spit of land formed by a loop of the Severn, a jewel in the necklace of the river. Almost an island, as a defensive site it has many more advantages than the site of the old Roman city which lay on the flat plane of open countryside beyond. Over time, fords would be replaced with bridges whose names reflect Shrewsbury's border identity: the English Bridge and the Welsh Bridge. For now, the Normans would take full advantage of the town's natural defences.

Roger De Montgomery built a Norman motte-and-bailey fortification overlooking the only place a person could enter the town without getting their feet wet. He also built an abbey at Shrewsbury for good measure which later became the setting for Edith Pargeter's fictional crime-fighting monk, Brother Cadfael. The Abbey as we see it today is only a remnant of a larger range of buildings that housed a monastic community. When Henry VIII began the Dissolution of the Monasteries in 1536 under powers given to him by parliament in the Act of Supremacy, the Abbey would have been expected to be destroyed as many in Shropshire were. The county is littered with ecclesiastical ruins with Haughmond, Buildwas, Lilleshall and Much Wenlock being the finest examples. Shrewsbury was fortunate because it performed a function beyond its monastic role. The main body of the church was used as a place of worship for members of the local

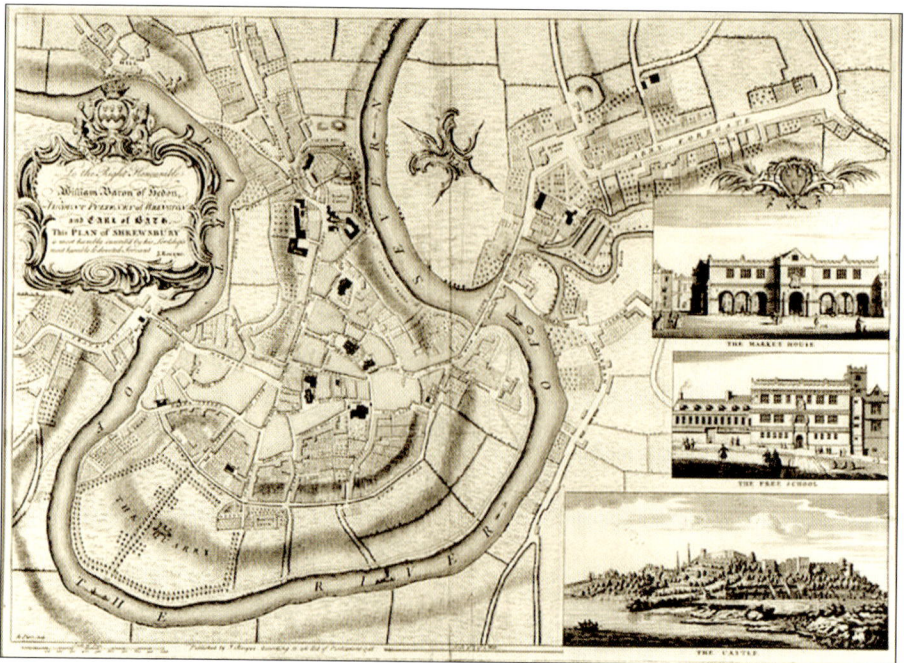

Shrewsbury, an etching by J. Rocque, 1746.

Above: The English Bridge.

Below: The Welsh Bridge.

Above: Shrewsbury Castle.

Below: Shrewsbury Abbey.

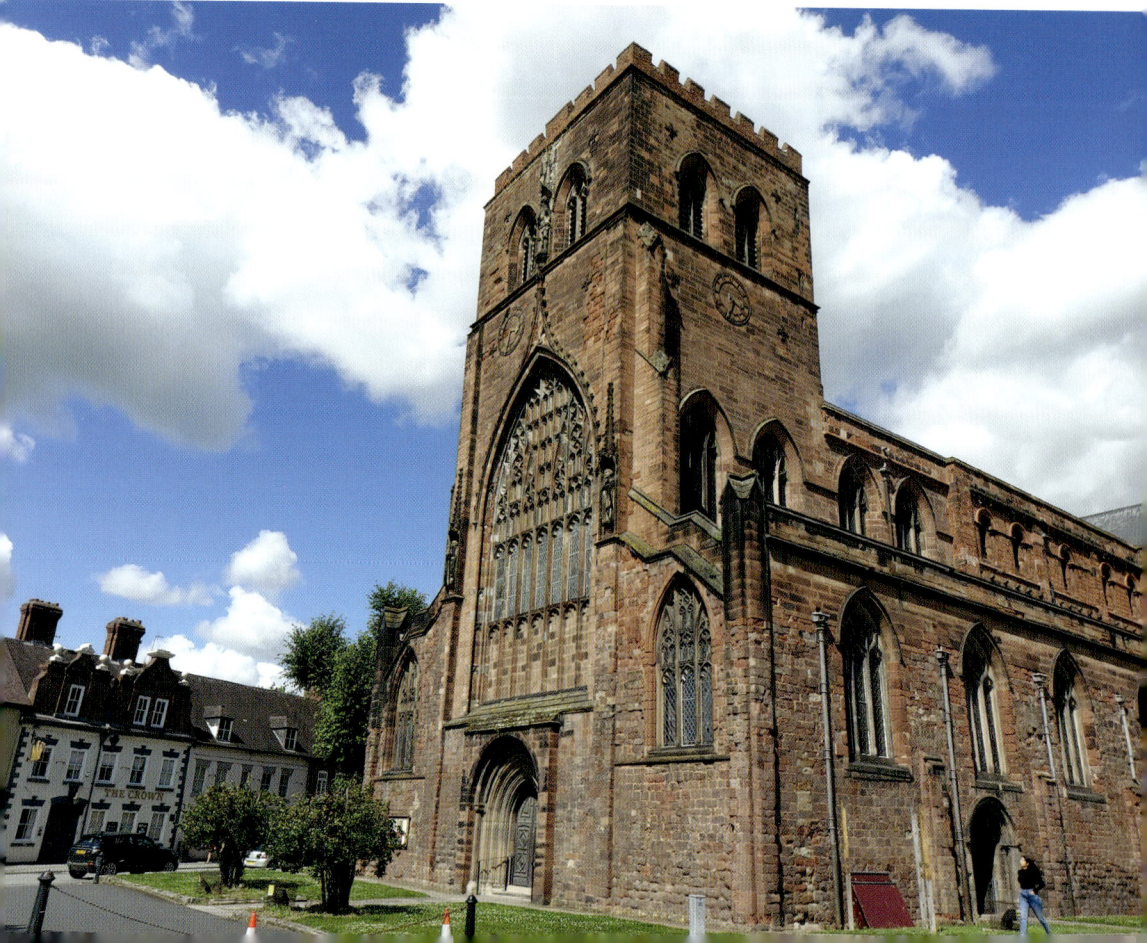

parish and as a consequence, it was only the outer range of buildings that were demolished under the King's brutal but lucrative programme of asset stripping.

On the northern outskirts of Shrewsbury where the suburbs give way to the countryside, Battlefield Church marks the site of a fierce fight that helped a King cling to power. Henry IV had been gifted the throne of England by a powerful cohort of knights who collaborated with him to wrestle the crown from Richard II on the promise of rewards. After the coronation, the favours did not materialise and the knights became disenchanted. On 21 July 1403, matters came to a head. Henry Hotspur had led an army of rebel knights to Shrewsbury hoping perhaps to recruit the King's son, Prince Hal, who was in residence there. Hotspur had mentored Hal and the two were friends, but when Hotspur's army arrived from the north they were dismayed to see not just the Prince's flag but also the King's colours flying over the town. Instead of a parley with the Prince, the knights were forced to square up to the full might of his father's forces. In the battle that followed, Prince Hal fought with distinction and contributed greatly to the King's ultimate victory. The circumstances leading up to the battle and Henry's eventual triumph are dramatised in one of Shakespeare's greatest works, *Henry IV Parts I & II*.

Battlefield Church.

By the Middle Ages, relations with the neighbours across the border had improved sufficiently for trade to start in earnest. By far the biggest trade was in wool. It was said that Shrewsbury's merchants grew wealthy on the backs of Welsh sheep. In the centre of the town's square stands the Old Market Hall where fleece and cloth were bought and sold. An impressive stone building, it reeks of ambition. The many merchant houses built nearby over the following centuries are testimony to the economic success of the town.

In the English Civil War, Shrewsbury was a Loyalist stronghold, as was Bridgnorth further downstream. Any town refusing to acknowledge the primacy of parliament over the crown could expect little leniency from Cromwell's Roundheads, yet Bridgnorth chose to resist. The Parliamentarian forces laid siege to the town, which fell after three weeks. Its castle was destroyed by cannon with only a fragment of the walls surviving today.

The Old Market Hall.

Shrewsbury fared much better. When the Roundheads came to call, someone left a gate unlocked in the town's fortified walls and Shrewsbury fell with little commotion. Whether it was an act of treachery or simple pragmatism is uncertain, but the residents would have been well aware of the fate of towns that held out against Cromwell's New Model Army. One thing is for sure, the result may have been a loss for the King but it was a victory for the cause of historic building preservation. A stroll around the streets of Shrewsbury is a living lesson in English architecture. Here, medieval timber-framed buildings jostle with Regency townhouses and examples of Victorian splendour. Locals and visitors are positively tripping over listed buildings.

This is the town in which Charles Darwin was born and he would recognise much of it today.

At the end of this book is a Darwin Walk so, if you're ever in town, bring it along and you too can walk in Darwin's footsteps.

Fish Street.

St John's Hill.

2

Shropshire – The Stone Watch

'Shropshire displays a greater variety of rocks than any other area of comparable size in the world.'

Dr Peter Toghill, University of Birmingham

In 1815, William Smith published his *Geological Map of England and Wales and Part of Scotland*. It was a timely publication as interest in geology was growing not only amongst the scientific community but also among the industrialists eager for the raw materials to drive their 'dark satanic mills'. It was the year of Bonaparte's defeat by the allies at Waterloo and Charles Darwin was six years old. The science of geology grew as Darwin grew and by the time he attended Edinburgh University, many scholars were specialising in the field. Smith's map is a remarkable achievement for its age but only hints at the geological complexity of Darwin's home county.

The county has an abundance of fossils particularly from the Silurian and Ordovician periods. The collection of fossils has long been a popular pastime but the question of what they represent has also been the cause of debate. Science recognises the fossil record as a glimpse into a bygone age, long before our ancestors first trod the earth, but that is an uncomfortable notion for some. In 1695 the pioneering geologist John Woodward dismissed the notion that fossils were merely patterns in the rock or designs placed there by God and posited that they were the remains of long-dead creatures.

It is the British scientist Arthur Holmes that we have to thank for our modern understanding of the age of the earth. Once described as 'the most famous British geologist you have never heard of', it was Holmes who combined an interest in geology with a fascination in the field of radioactivity to reach some remarkable conclusions. In 1910, Holmes developed a technique of calculating the age of rocks and minerals using radiometric dating. Three years later in his book *The Age of the Earth*, Holmes dated the age of our home planet at a conservative 1.6 billion years. By 1946, following refinements and improvements to the technique, the consensus amongst the scientific community was a far greater age of 4.5 billion years.

Though radiometric dating was over half a century in the future, Darwin's perspective and astute sense of observation enabled him to see in the landscape anomalies that fed his curiosity, anomalies that could only occur over time on a grand scale that contributed to his great idea, an idea that subsequent decades of scientific progress has been able to validate.

Holmes' contribution to our understanding of the earth didn't end with a start date; he broadened his study of radioactivity to explore the consequences of the heat emitted from the earth's core and suggested that radioactive waves were the engine behind the movement of giant tectonic plates on the earth's surface.

As Holmes was able to prove, the slow, inexorable dance of these plates has caused the rise and fall of mountain ranges, the formation of oceans and the creation and destruction of whole continents. The landmass of Shropshire, or at least parts of it, has been on an incredible journey beginning some 60 degrees south of the equator, gathering evidence of the ages along the way. As a consequence, Shropshire boasts ten of the thirteen recognised geological periods in its landscape. No surprise then that Shropshire became a magnet for pioneering Victorian geologists such as Murchison, Lapworth and Callaway who plundered county place names as they founded systems that have remained in geological textbooks to this day such as Caradoc, Wenlock and Ludlow, and Shropshire continues to provide a teaching ground for new generations of geologists.

As you approach the county from the north, west or east, the largest landmark is The Wrekin Hill. Rising some 407 metres above sea level, it looms up from the flat, North Shropshire Plain. The hill is a popular destination for walkers, offering as it

The Wrekin Hill, Shropshire's most impressive landmark, viewed from the nearby Ercall.

does spectacular views in all directions, and along its ridge is evidence of ancient, Iron Age habitation. A mile to the west lies the village of Rushton and evidence of a far older age. The stone beneath Rushton was formed in the Precambrian Age between 700 and 545 million years ago.

Alongside The Wrekin is its little sister, The Ercall Hill, and here, in an abandoned quarry, the transition from Precambrian to Cambrian is visible. A dramatic feature known as the Ercall Unconformity shows the phenomenon that became known as the Cambrian Explosion, on a geological scale, a sudden and spectacular increase of life on Earth. One of the largest and more unusual fossils at The Ercall demonstrates the extent to which the earth's surface has traversed the globe. 500 million years ago when its land mass was in the southern hemisphere, Shropshire had a coastline. Waves lapped on its beaches and today, high up on a quarry ledge, the stone slope is embossed with the ripples of that sandy seabed, some 60 miles from the nearest coastline.

On an expedition with the geologist Adam Sedgwick to the Welsh valley of Cwm Idwal in 1831, Darwin had seen evidence of this contortion, observing marine fossils in rock strata many metres above sea level. As remarkable as these

The Ercall Unconformity can be seen at the centre of the picture at the highest point of the exposed quarry face.

The fossilised ripples of an ancient seabed as if the tide had just gone out.

finds were, Cwm Idwal offered another insight that explained the very making of the landscape itself. It was staring the two men in the face but they couldn't see it then. So fixed were they on finding fossils that as Darwin admitted, 'neither of us a saw a trace of the wonderful glacial phenomena all around us'. Ten years later, Darwin returned to Cwm Idwal with a new perspective and a fresh pair of eyes, enlightened by his experience on the *Beagle*. Here were the 'plainly scored rocks, the perched boulders' that he and Sedgwick had seen a decade earlier but now in a moment of clarity, he looked again at the bowl of the valley and the story came to life. He imagined it full to the brim with solid, glacial ice which, over millennia, carved the landscape beneath its mass. The positioning of the 'perched boulders' that Darwin had seen, resting a short distance from the lake's edge, could now be explained. In 1842, Darwin recorded his findings concluding that:

They must have been pitched into their present position with great force; and as the two upright thin tabular pieces are placed transversely to the gentle slope on which they stand, it is scarcely possible to conceive that they could have been rolled down from the mountain behind them; one is led, therefore, to conclude that they were dropped nearly vertically from a height into their present places.

Darwin suggested that having been carried on the surface of the glacier, a fissure had opened up and the boulders had fallen 'through a crevice in the ice'. This phenomenon creates what are known as supraglacial erratics. It was suddenly startlingly obvious to the extent that he wrote 'a house burnt down by fire did not tell its story more plainly than did this valley'.

The land falls and rises and the jostling of tectonic plates pushes great mountains into the sky but Darwin realised that ice and water are accomplished engineers too.

To the south of The Wrekin, Wenlock Edge rolls south-west. Another famous landmark, Wenlock Edge has been immortalised in verse by A. E. Houseman

Darwin's Boulders at Cwm Idwal.

Adam Sedgwick.

whose words were the inspiration for music by Ralph Vaughn Williams, the grand-nephew of Darwin. A Silurian escarpment, this dramatic limestone ridge is riven with the fossils of marine creatures that once inhabited coral reefs.

To the west of Wenlock Edge, the town of Church Stretton lies in what is known as the Stretton Fault. This is the heart of the South Shropshire Hills, an area rich not only in geology but folklore too. Legend has it that beneath the Shropshire Hills rests the Anglo-Saxon nobleman Wild Edric with his wife, Lady Godda, guarded by his loyal army. Having fought a successful guerrilla campaign against the occupying Norman forces, he eventually swore allegiance to them. In anger, the locals laid a curse on Edric that banished him to a realm beneath the hills only to rise whenever the country is in peril. Centuries later, some swore that Edric tapped on the stone walls of nearby Snailbeach Mine to lead the burrowers to the richest seams.

In this part of the South Shropshire Hills it is possible to journey through the late Precambrian, Cambrian and Ordovician periods to the Silurian, some 90 million years or so of earth's history in around 13 miles, as the crow flies.

To the north of the Shropshire Hills, the land flattens as far as the Cheshire Plain. From Shrewsbury and out towards Market Drayton, Permian and Triassic sandstone can be found. Sandstone outcrops such as Nesscliffe, Pimhill and Grinshill punctuate the flat topography. Close to the village of Prees in North Shropshire, the Jurassic Period is represented.

Evidence of the earth's more recent history can be seen in an area known as the Meres and Mosses, close to the town of Ellesmere in Shropshire's 'Lake District'. Here, pools and peat bogs are evidence of the last great ice age. The sheer weight

Above: Nipstone, one of many dramatic, rocky outcrops along The Stiperstones.

Below: On the horizon, Caradoc Hill, site of an Iron Age hill fort.

The town of Church Stretton nestles in the Shropshire Hills.

of ice left hollows in the soft ground and as the glaciers receded, they deposited meltwater and created the jewels of standing water that give the area its distinctive character.

Over time, and during Shropshire's epic journey, rich mineral deposits have been laid down. The Snailbeach Mine is located beneath a ridge of the Shropshire Hills to the west of Church Stretton called the Stiperstones. The ruins of the engine room, offices and forge have been preserved and are cared for by the Shropshire Mines Trust who host guided walks into the mines. Stepping stooped into the narrow passages, it is possible to get a sense of the grim working conditions the ancient miners laboured under. The Romans mined lead in this area and production at the mines didn't peak until 1860.

The predominantly rural landscape of modern Shropshire belies its industrious past. The mineral deposits, coalfields and abundant woodlands provided the raw

Above: The entrance to Snailbeach Mine.

Below: The original forge is on the left beside a reconstruction of the pithead.

materials for industrial activity for many centuries, albeit on a small scale until a dramatic breakthrough by the ironmaster Abraham Darby in 1709. Darby had relocated to Coalbrookdale in Shropshire from Bristol. It was a shrewd move as the county had all the raw materials he could possibly need. Coalbrookdale is situated to the east of The Wrekin in a vale adjacent to a larger gorge which was created at the end of the last ice age when a great volume of melting ice forced a new, southerly path for what we now know as the River Severn. This glacial legacy provided Darby with a thoroughfare for boats to exchange goods and raw materials to the Severn Estuary and the wider world beyond.

In a second-hand furnace, Darby perfected a means of smelting iron with coke. More robust than charcoal, coke allowed greater quantities of ore to be loaded into the top of the furnace. During his experiments, Darby stuffed the keyhole of his workroom with rags to frustrate prying eyes; yet when the method was

The Ironbridge, opened in 1781, the first of its kind in the world.

perfected, he did not apply for a patent, perhaps a mark of his Quaker generosity. As a consequence of Darby's breakthrough, output increased at a previously unimaginable rate and the Industrial Revolution began. As output grew, so did the skills of the iron casters: pots, rails, ornate fountains and all manner of goods were cast in iron and the material played many of the roles that plastic does today. A new class appeared in British society, the Industrialist. In the generation that followed were the entrepreneurs Boulton and Watt, friends and collaborators of Darwin's grandfathers, Erasmus Darwin and Josiah Wedgwood. And all of this enterprise was founded on a geological legacy writ large on the landscape of Shropshire and billions of years in the making.

The most remarkable things can be achieved, given time. Dogs and cats, racehorses and racing pigeons have all, to a greater or lesser extent, been fashioned

The furnace at Coalbrookdale where Abraham Darby I perfected the process of smelting iron with coke. (With permission of The Ironbridge Gorge Museum Trust)

at our whim since their domestication began around 40,000 years ago. We have adapted them to suit our purposes and tastes through the process of selective breeding. The change is most dramatic in the case of dogs. Compare a chihuahua with a Siberian husky and it's hard to imagine they have the same ancestor. During the period of research that eventually led to his greatest work, *On the Origin of Species*, Darwin took time to seek out expert breeders, hoping to gain a greater understanding of what changes can occur over time.

Some would place the age of the earth at a mere 4,000 years old, according to calculations based on figures extrapolated from biblical text by Archbishop Ussher in 1650. On the voyage of the *Beagle*, Darwin observed in nature what he considered to be subtle adaptations in animals only possible over years measured not in thousands but millions. 4,000 years is simply not enough time for natural laws to produce the startling variety of life on Earth through so many tiny, incremental changes. Darwin's 'Theory on the Origin of Species' is complete nonsense without the benefit of time. This perceived anomaly perhaps accounts for the disproportionate number of attacks on Darwin's theories more than any other scientific figure, by those whose faith is founded on the account of creation found in the book of Genesis. Darwin had chosen to look outside The Book and the evidence of pre-history was right on his doorstep. He was fortunate to have grown up in a county with a geological clock that started ticking long before Man's arrival. We know that within a few miles of the family home in Shrewsbury lie stones with stories that began over 700 million years ago. In the hills of South Shropshire we can see the fossils of creatures that swam in long-lost oceans and nearby The Wrekin, formed from lava and volcanic ash that tells of more turbulent times.

The world, as many scientists had come to realise, was in a state of constant contortion, rising and falling, shifting and drifting; a world in motion. Time makes all things possible.

Darwin's vision of transformation by minor adjustments over millennia was built on solid foundations, the rocks of the ages. So, the true age of the earth as it is illustrated in the landscape of Shropshire becomes the first of the Three Pillars.

3

Meet the Ancestors

It is a remarkable fact that Charles Darwin formulated a simple, compelling and enduring theory that explained the painstaking process of the transfer of traits across generations, resulting in the spectacular variety of life on Earth without even knowing what a gene was. In *Origin* Darwin states plainly that 'the laws governing inheritance are quite unknown; no one can say why the same peculiarity in different individuals of the same species is sometimes inherited and sometimes not so'. It was the work of the Augustinian friar Gregor Mendel that laid the foundations for our present understanding of the science of genetics. But Darwin had no access to Mendel's papers as the monk's work didn't become widely known until the turn of the twentieth century, more than three decades after they were first published.

To solve the great riddle, Darwin simply used curiosity and a keen eye. He relied on the evidence he could observe, meticulously recording his findings to amass a wealth of evidence to support his wonderful idea. It is by any measure an audacious notion for its time but a glance back along his family tree reveals two characters who were well used to ruffling feathers: Darwin's grandfathers, Erasmus Darwin and Josiah Wedgwood. Born in 1731, Erasmus was a physician, poet, philosopher and inventor. He developed a copying machine and a speaking machine, and the mechanical means he devised to steer carriages is still used today in the automotive industry.

Erasmus Darwin's radical views were something of an irritant to the church in his home town of Lichfield. Biographer Desmond King-Hele noted that 'his family coat of arms consisted of three scallop shells. What a good idea to add the motto E conchis omnia, or "everything from shells"'. Darwin painted the emblem and motto on the side of his carriage, much to the annoyance of the canon of Lichfield Cathedral. The senior Darwin's antics were made all the more galling by the proximity of his house to the cathedral, which was just around the corner. As James Kier, a close friend of Darwin's grandfather, noted 'he paid little regard to authority'.

Erasmus Darwin was highly esteemed as a poet and is said to have influenced the English Romantics who followed him such as Wordsworth, Keats, Coleridge, Byron and the Shelleys. He is best remembered for his book *Zoonomia*, an early evolutionist piece that speculated that life on Earth changed over time and was not fixed, in contrast to the biblical account. It was a work that Darwin greatly admired in his university years but when he revisited the book a decade or so later he was 'much disappointed, the proportion of speculation being so large to the facts given'.

Josiah Wedgwood was a year older than Erasmus and the founding father of the Wedgwood pottery dynasty. His innovations in the production of pottery were driven by an interest in chemistry and he experimented for several years in the manufacture of porcelain. Wedgwood's pottery found favour in the upper echelons of society including the royal court: Queen Charlotte purchased a tea set 'complete with candlesticks and fruit baskets'.

In 1775, after years of research, Wedgwood developed a technique that entailed the application of finely detailed reliefs in white clay onto pots and vases. Metallic oxides were then used to provide a matte-coloured background, most commonly a classical pale blue which to this day is referred to as Wedgwood Blue. The pottery became known as jasperware and established a worldwide reputation for Wedgwood who could also count European royalty among his clientele. Wedgwood was a pioneer of sales and marketing techniques familiar to us today such as direct mail, money-back guarantees, free delivery, celebrity endorsement, illustrated catalogues and even 'buy one get one free'. He was also a radical and a passionate voice in the anti-slavery movement, producing an abolitionist medal to publicise the cause.

It was Erasmus who instigated the creation of a group of like-minded souls who became known as the Lunar Men. They met for dinner and conversation at each other's houses on the Monday nearest the full moon to assist them on their homeward journey. It was a meeting of great minds at a time of innovation, excitement and infinite possibilities. The Industrial Revolution that was sparked in nearby Coalbrookdale was gathering momentum and the Lunar Men were at its heart. Lunar HQ was Soho House, the home of the industrialist Matthew Boulton, who would later partner with the Scottish engineer James Watt to corner the market in the steam engines that pumped floodwater from the lucrative Cornish tin mines.

The bond of friendship between Darwin and Wedgwood was sealed when two of their offspring married. Robert Darwin married Susannah Wedgwood in 1796.

Above left: Erasmus Darwin, founder of the Lunar Men.

Above right: Josiah Wedgwood, founder of the great pottery dynasty.

The combined wealth of the two branches of the family was considerable and laid a solid foundation for Darwin's future comfort, but idleness was never an option. The Wedgwoods and the Darwins were industrious folk and there was an expectation that young Charles would continue the family tradition and take an active and productive role in Shrewsbury society.

As we have heard, Darwin sympathised with his half-cousin Francis Dalton in the belief that 'education & environment produce only a small effect on the mind of anyone' and that 'most of our qualities are innate'. In the twentieth century, the pioneering sociologist Bourdieu argued by contrast that the richer our childhoods, in terms of exposure to culture and experiences beyond the day-to-day family routine, the better our chances in life. The contribution that family and social life endow on a child's intellectual development and social mobility can be significant. A child who is allowed to participate in discussions and to question, a child who is exposed to the arts and culture, a child who is supported and encouraged is a child with a distinct advantage over one who is born into more humble circumstances, devoid of intellectual and social stimulation. Bourdieu called these factors social and cultural capital. It's a phenomenon that is distilled in the adage 'Give me a child until he is seven and I will show you the man.'

Darwin was lucky. A simple accident of birth placed him in a family environment that was both stimulating and challenging and with such capital in the bank, he would have been foolish not to invest it. Though he may have faltered through his teens and early twenties, he most certainly did take advantage and combined with his innate passion for natural history was able to leave an enduring legacy.

Above left: Matthew Boulton, industrialist and entrepreneur.

Above right: Robert Darwin.

4

Life at The Mount

Robert and Susannah Darwin moved to Shrewsbury from Lichfield in 1787 to establish a medical practice and here they resided in a fashionable house on The Crescent. In fairly short order, Robert had laid the foundations of a successful career and soon set about laying the foundations of a family home. The location chosen was a short distance from the town centre, across the Welsh Bridge. Robert built an impressive house on raised ground overlooking the suburb of Frankwell with the spire of St Alkmund's and the tower of St Julian's churches across the river in the distance. It was close to open countryside with extensive gardens that sloped gently to the east and more precipitously to the north where they dropped down to the banks of the Severn. The view from the rear of the house has changed little and the meadows nearby are now a local nature reserve, Doctors Field.

The Crescent, Shrewsbury.

Above: The Mount.

Below: Doctor's Field Nature Reserve.

Charles Robert Darwin was born on 12 February 1809 and joined siblings Marianne, Caroline, Susan and Erasmus, or 'Ras' as he was known in the family, in what must have been a bustling household. In an autobiographical fragment written in 1838, Darwin had scant recollections of his earliest years. There was a trip to the seaside at the age of four, the first of many such trips to the Welsh coast, and he does recall the illuminations that celebrated the allied victory at Waterloo in 1815.

Darwin showed a fascination for the natural world from an early age. By the time he attended his first school, he had developed a keenness for collecting 'chiefly seals, franks etc., but also pebbles and minerals'. Darwin was eight years old and in his own words 'had smattered in botany' and was 'very keen on gardening'. Darwin flitted from one scientific obsession to another in his formative years whilst retaining a little of everything as he went, rather like a bee buzzing through a garden, gathering pollen from every flower it visits. Darwin remembers the desire 'to know something about every pebble in front of the hall door'. He later affirms that 'it was my earliest and only geological aspiration at that time'.

By the age of ten, a new interest overtook the fascination with stones and minerals. During a three-week family holiday at Plas Edwards in Tywyn on the Welsh coast, the sighting of several insects and moths that Darwin was certain could not be found in Shropshire sparked an interest in entomology and a desire to collect all the dead specimens he could find, for having discussed the matter with his sister, he had concluded that it would not be right 'to kill insects for the sake of making a collection'.

However, in no time at all, it was the habits of birds that had grabbed his attention. He began to make notes on the subject and filled with enthusiasm wondered 'why every gentleman did not become an ornithologist'. Towards the end of his school life, he was assisting his brother Ras as he undertook experiments in a homemade chemistry laboratory in an outbuilding of the family home. As Darwin observed in later life, it was a practical demonstration of 'the meaning of experimental science'. When word of their chemical capers reached school, Darwin's contemporaries nicknamed him 'Gas'.

As a child, he enjoyed long, solitary walks and on one occasion whilst circumnavigating the steep defensive mound of Shrewsbury Castle, lost his footing and fell several feet. It was not the accident itself that left a lasting impression on Darwin but that 'the number of thoughts which passed through my mind during this very short, but sudden and wholly unexpected fall, was astonishing, and seems hardly compatible with what physiologists have, I believe, proved about each thought requiring quite an appreciable amount of time'. Perhaps his young life had flashed before his eyes. Contemplative walks were to play an important part in Darwin's work pattern when he later settled at Down House in the village of Downe in Kent, now in the care of English Heritage. At Down, it is possible to see the study where he wrote and to stroll along his 'thinking path' at the edge of the garden. The path forms a loop through a small copse of trees and

Darwin was in the habit of taking regular breaks from writing to lose himself in the sounds of nature and crystallise his thoughts before returning to write in the study. It's a widely acknowledged practice. Friedrich Nietzsche wrote that 'all truly great thoughts are conceived by walking' or to use the Latin phrase, *Solvitur Ambulando* – it is solved by walking. His childhood home, The Mount, had a similar path that zig-zagged from the terrace at the rear of the house down through the steep escarpment, past a red-brick ice house to the river below. A remnant of this path and the ice house survives to this day and is presently in the ownership of the Shropshire Wildlife Trust.

Robert and Susannah kept diaries containing detailed notes on the success or otherwise of planting in the grounds, kitchen gardens and greenhouses at The Mount. It is this early indoctrination in the disciplines of observation and experimentation that would prove invaluable to Darwin when he committed to the life of a naturalist.

A remnant of the Thinking Path. (With permission of The Shropshire Wildlife Trust)

Botany, horticulture, geology, mineralogy, entomology, ornithology, chemistry and cognitive psychology, by the time he reached university, Darwin had already been a very busy bee. In truth, some of these interests were only passing fancies but there was an accumulative effect. His time at Edinburgh would add marine biology to the growing list, by which time the path ahead was clear, if only to Charles. Darwin was displaying the traits of the polymath, one who is not content with one specialism. This eclectic approach echoed that of his grandfathers and their friends in the Lunar Society who felt no constraint to their curiosity. It was an ethos rooted in a common bond of religious nonconformity.

The Darwin family's relationship with religion was not conventional. His grandfather Erasmus had enjoyed sparring with the canon of Lichfield Cathedral on theological matters and had called into question the orthodox view of creation and the fixed nature of diversity in his work *Zoonomia*. Darwin's father, Robert, was not known for his piety and his mother, Susannah, had been brought up in the Unitarian movement. For the Unitarians, there was less emphasis on the supernatural, the Trinity, the Father, Son and Holy Ghost; theirs was a more grounded belief. God was demystified and curiosity unbounded by dogma. Nonconformists, like the Lunar Men, employed reason and logic to solve the mysteries of the ages. Each discovery was a potential gateway to greater understanding and it didn't do their bank balances any harm either. The Lunar Men demonstrated that curiosity could be lucrative.

The Darwins were part of a rebellion that had begun some centuries earlier. In the sixteenth century, a religious movement challenged the primacy of the Catholic Church. Across mainland Europe figures such as John Calvin and Martin Luther argued against the right of the Catholic Church to define man's relationship with God. It was a call for a more egalitarian faith where the bible was put into the hands of the people and not guarded jealously by priests. Henry VIII was challenging the status quo too, though perhaps for reasons less rooted in theological discourse. His failure to persuade the pope to grant him a divorce from his first wife, Catherine of Aragon, to free him to marry Anne Boleyn culminated in the establishment of the Church of England and the marginalising of the Catholic faith. Over a century later an Act of Parliament in 1661 defined the notion of nonconformity. The Test and Corporation Act demanded that not only peers and MPs but schoolmasters, clergy, students at Oxford and Cambridge and members of local corporations swear an oath upholding the position of the King as head of the Church of England. The alternative was a loss of civil rights. The Act threatened those who would not conform with a fine or even imprisonment. A brief respite followed with the coronation of James II but his replacement by William of Orange in 1688 heralded another age of suspicion and religious intolerance.

The more conciliatory Act of Toleration passed in 1689 exempted Baptists, Quakers and Presbyterians from 'the penalties of certain laws' but not Catholics and Unitarians. And still the flame of Unitarianism burned. The first Unitarian church in England was founded in 1774 with the support of Joseph Priestly, a contemporary of Erasmus Darwin and Josiah Wedgwood and a fellow member of the Lunar Men. Being barred from the old universities did not impede their intellectual development – far from it. The old universities were still teaching a curriculum that had changed little in generations and majored heavily on the classics. Priestly set up a school in Warrington with 'a lively new curriculum for

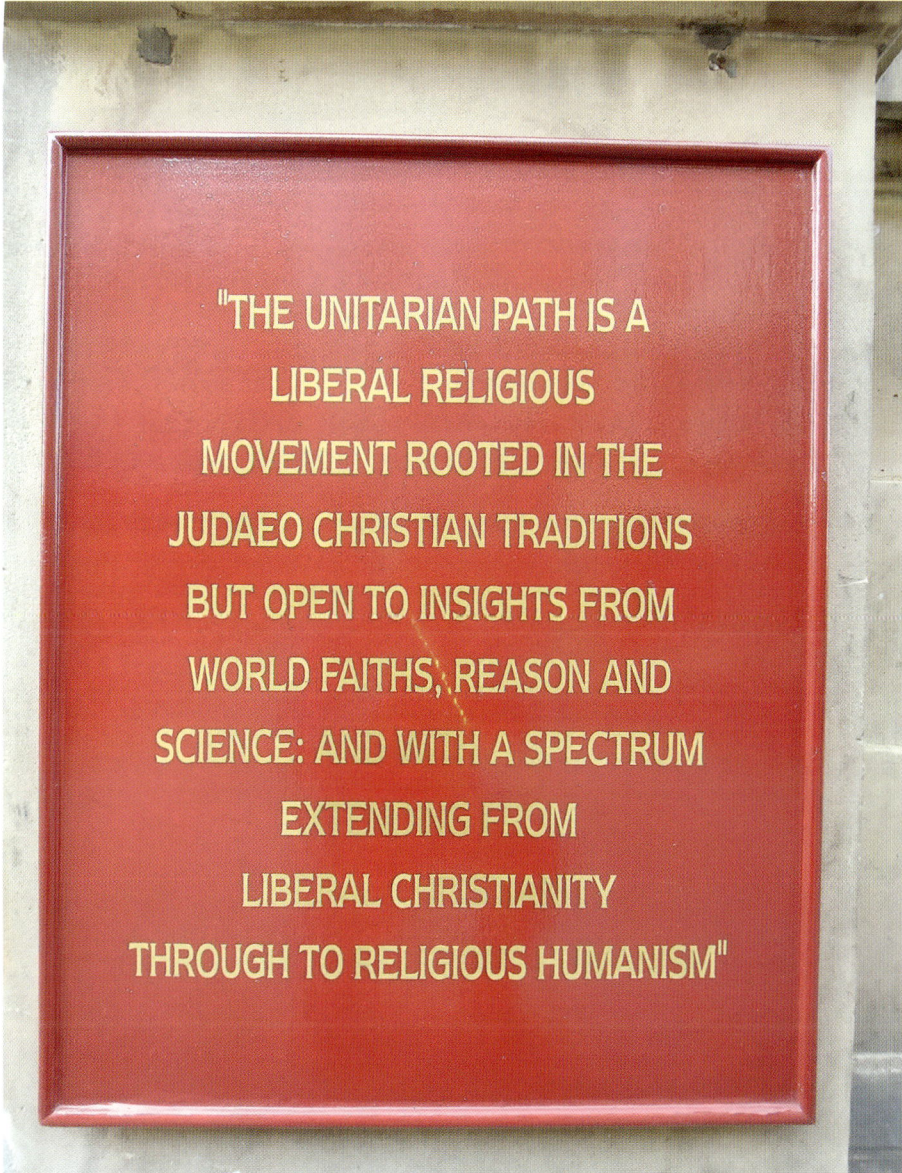

"THE UNITARIAN PATH IS A LIBERAL RELIGIOUS MOVEMENT ROOTED IN THE JUDAEO CHRISTIAN TRADITIONS BUT OPEN TO INSIGHTS FROM WORLD FAITHS, REASON AND SCIENCE: AND WITH A SPECTRUM EXTENDING FROM LIBERAL CHRISTIANITY THROUGH TO RELIGIOUS HUMANISM"

The plaque on the Unitarian Church.

girls as well as boys' that included a science course. At Priestley's school, students were actively encouraged to challenge their tutors and think for themselves. Science and experimentation were considered at least as important as the classics and there was a real sense that curiosity would lead to enlightenment. One could argue that the mercantile and scientific success of nonconformists was not achieved despite sanctions but because of them.

Nonconformists played a prominent role in the technological and societal seismic shift that occurred from the seventeenth century onwards. Abraham Darby, the founding father of the Industrial Revolution, was a Quaker and his grandson, Abraham Darby III, built the world's first iron bridge. Elizabeth Fry, also a Quaker, was an English prison and social reformer. Darwin's maternal grandfather, Josiah Wedgwood, was a Unitarian and in the twentieth century, Tim Berners-Lee, also a Unitarian, was responsible for sparking the networked revolution with the creation of the World Wide Web.

The Unitarian ethos underpinned Darwin's first formal schooling which was at the home of the Revd George Case, the minister at Shrewsbury's Unitarian Church. The figures who preached from the pulpit of this church were not authoritarian. Unitarians preached of our inherent humanity and individual worth when the established church spoke of inherent guilt and innate depravity. The Unitarian creed spoke of the universal salvation of all souls, a view opposed to the notion of original sin.

A plaque on the outer wall of the Unitarian Church on Shrewsbury High Street defines the movement as grounded in the Judeo-Christian tradition but 'open to insights from World Faith, reason and science'. Not only was Darwin able to think outside the box but he also had permission to look outside The Book. Unitarianism freed Darwin to ask questions that others were content to leave unanswered or simply pass off as the will of the divine. With innate curiosity and unshackled by any theological constraints, Darwin boarded HMS *Beagle* with an open, enquiring mind. And so, the liberal and enlightened Unitarian Path becomes the second of the Three Pillars.

5

School Days

Darwin was initially home-schooled by his elder sister Caroline, who was 'extremely kind, clever and zealous'. In comparison to his younger sister Catherine, he 'was much slower in learning'. Darwin confesses to having been in many ways a naughty boy and one who resented Caroline's attempts to improve him. For some time afterwards, he would steel himself before entering a room he knew Caroline to be in wondering 'what will she blame me for now?'.

In the spring of 1817 Darwin began his short spell at the day school run by the Revd Case. Darwin's mother, Susannah, had fallen ill at the start of the year and as

Caroline Darwin.

the months went by, her condition began to worsen. She died on 15 July. The loss of his mother would have clearly been upsetting but in later life, Darwin could only recollect 'her deathbed, her black velvet gown and her curiously constructed work-table'. This forgetfulness Darwin suggests was a consequence of his sister's 'great grief never being able to speak about her or mention her name; and partly her previous invalid state'. Robert was now a widower and though only fifty-one years of age, never remarried and lived to the age of eighty-two.

Case's home was close to the town's park known as The Quarry. As the name suggests there was indeed a quarry at the site but the stone was of poor quality and was abandoned. The hollow that the stonemasons left behind became flooded and later the surrounding ground was planted into formal gardens and is now known as The Dingle. As a child, Darwin 'took great delight … in fishing for newts in the quarry pool'.

Darwin was only with Case for a year before moving across town to Shrewsbury School. Founded in 1552 by royal charter under Edward VI, the school occupied impressive buildings close to Shrewsbury Castle. The street that runs between the two is known as Castle Gates to underline their strategic position. Darwin recalls little of his time under the tutelage of the Revd Case but Shrewsbury School made a more lasting, though not altogether positive, impression on him.

The pool in the Dingle.

By the time Darwin attended Shrewsbury, it was under the direction of its thirteenth headmaster, Dr Samuel Butler. Butler was a classics scholar educated at Rugby and later St John's College, Cambridge. It is Butler whom English public school pupils have to thank for the system of placing older boys in a position of authority over their younger peers. One might describe it as peer mentoring but it was often open to abuse by the school bully, epitomised by the fictional character Flashman in Thomas Hughes' 1857 novel *Tom Brown's Schooldays*, a book set in Butler's alma mater, Rugby. The regime at Shrewsbury was in marked contrast to the more relaxed routine to which Darwin had become accustomed.

Darwin's entry in the school register. (Courtesy of Shrewsbury School)

The atmosphere was austere and brutal. Fights between boys were common, though surprisingly Butler appears to have turned a blind eye. Perhaps he thought the practice to be character building.

Even though the family home was less than a mile's walk away, Darwin boarded at the school so that he had 'the great advantage of living the life of a true school-boy'. It's clear from Darwin's later recollections that any advantage was minimal. Life was tough for boarders and Darwin shared the same deprivations as the other boys. Food was meagre, only adding to the misery. It was a running joke between pupils that the initials 'S.B.' carved above the gateway to the headmaster's house which neighboured the school stood not for 'Samuel Butler' but for 'stale bread' or perhaps 'stinking beef'. Despite this, Butler is credited with turning around the fortunes of the school that had been in decline under previous headmasters.

Darwin made several friends at school and one acquaintance named Garnett was responsible for playing a prank on him that he was to remember many years later. It is possible that Garnett's father was well respected amongst the merchants of the town as his son was able to obtain goods on credit with no formal

Shrewsbury Library, formerly Shrewsbury School.

The initials of Darwin's headmaster, Samuel Butler.

transaction. This was an arrangement that Garnett omitted to mention to Darwin when the two were out and about in town. Darwin saw how his schoolmate could walk into a shop, help himself to an item and simply walk out without challenge. Naturally curious, Darwin asked how this was possible? Garnett responded that the hat he was wearing was his father's and so long as he tipped it in a particular fashion towards the shopkeeper, he did not need coins to obtain goods. Seeing that his friend was taken in, Garnett suggested that Darwin put on the hat and give it a try. Darwin 'gladly accepted the generous offer', dutifully donned the chapeau and strode purposefully into a nearby cake shop (years later, Darwin even remembered which cake shop). He asked for some cakes which the shopkeeper handed over, at which point Darwin moved the hat in the manner prescribed by Garnett and proceeded to walk out of the shop without paying. At this point 'the shop-man made a rush at me, so I dropped the cakes and ran away for dear life'. Garnett, who had been waiting outside and watching with interest, greeted his chum with 'shouts of laughter'.

Darwin used the proximity of The Mount to regularly slip home to visit his family after the school day was finished, returning to his dormitory before it was locked up for the night. There were occasions when he would cut it a bit fine but he was young and fleet of foot and if he felt in danger of missing lockdown he would 'pray earnestly to God'. He attributed any success he had to the latter and not to his athletic prowess and 'marvelled how generally I was aided'. The frequent trips home were advantageous, allowing Darwin to keep up 'home affections and interests'.

Reflecting on his character during his schooldays, Darwin remembers having 'strong and diversified tastes, much zeal for whatever interested me, and a keen pleasure in understanding any complex subject or thing'. The young schoolboy

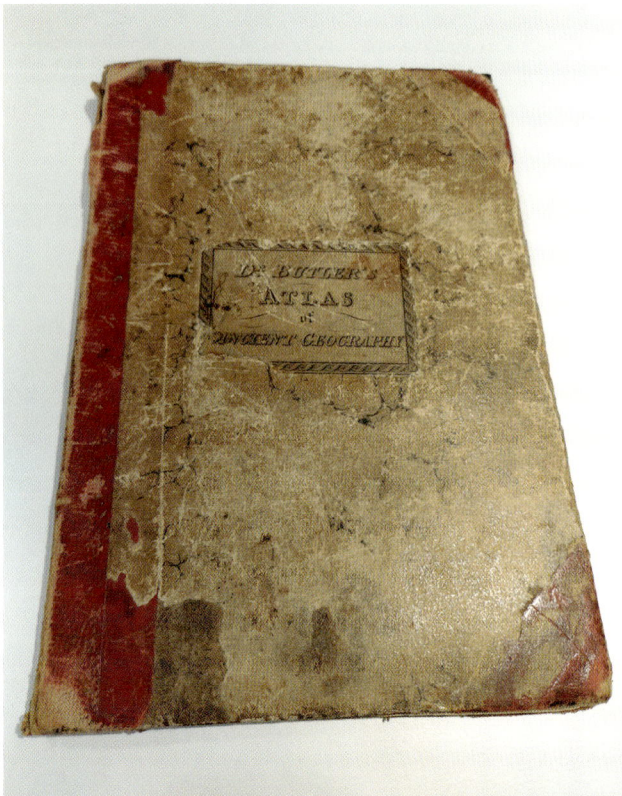

Darwin's copy of the school atlas. (Courtesy of Shrewsbury School)

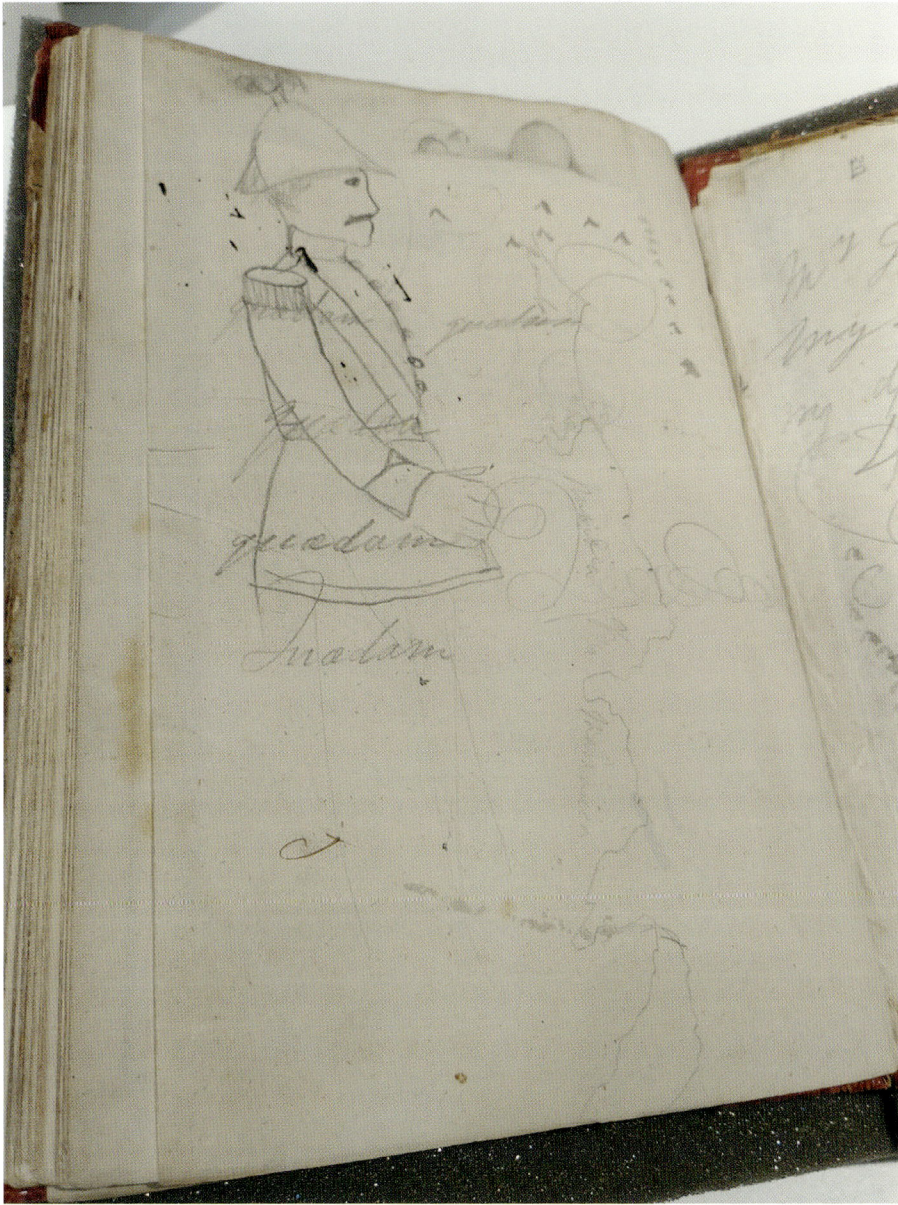

Inside the atlas is a doodle by the young Charles of a military figure. (Courtesy of Shrewsbury School)

enjoyed reading poetry and would also 'sit for hours in an old window in the thick walls of the school' consuming 'the historical plays of Shakespeare'.

Butler was a stickler for the classics, which was hardly surprising considering his academic interests back at Rugby. Darwin was required to spend countless hours learning the verse of Virgil and Homer by rote and by his own account, with little or

The Music Room inside Shrewsbury Library.

no lasting effect. He could learn '40 or 50 lines … whilst I was in morning chapel; but this exercise was utterly useless for every verse was forgotten within 48 hours'.

Darwin spent seven years at Shrewsbury School and on leaving was considered 'neither high nor low in it'; both his masters and his father agreed that Charles was 'a very ordinary boy'. On one thing Darwin was certain. Writing in May 1876, he states that 'nothing could have been worse for the development of my mind than Dr Butler's school'.

Right: Original library shelves and ancient books now at Shrewsbury School's current campus. (Courtesy of Shrewsbury School)

Below: Many boys left their mark on Shrewsbury School.

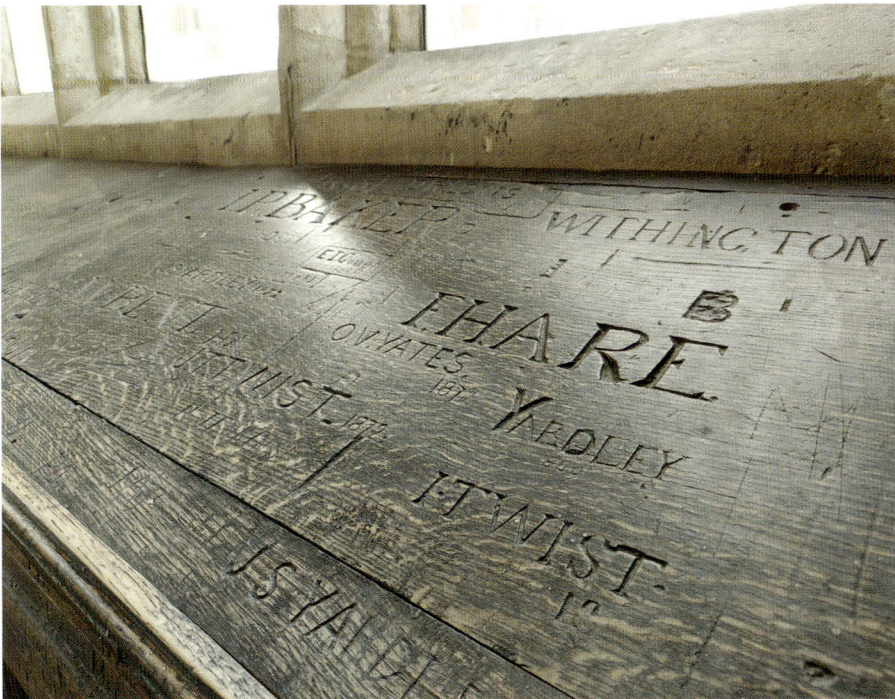

6

Edinburgh – A Doctor's Life?

'As I was doing no good at school, my father wisely took me away earlier than usual, and sent me (October 1825) to Edinburgh University.'
Autobiography, Charles Darwin, 1876

Robert Darwin sent his son to study medicine in Edinburgh where his brother Ras was beginning a final year of external hospital study, having previously been at Cambridge. Ras was looking forward to it, commenting 'It will be very pleasant our being together, we shall be as cosy as possible.' It appears that the brothers were only studying medicine out of some sense of duty to their father. Darwin did not believe that Ras 'ever really intended to practice'. Ras did begin a career in medicine after leaving Edinburgh but ill health brought it to an abrupt end and Robert provided the financial means for his eldest son to retire at the age of twenty-six, an arrangement that Ras found 'very agreeable'.

Charles found the lectures at Edinburgh 'intolerably dull'. It was not just the monotony of lecturers that put Darwin off the study of medicine. He attended the operating theatre and observed 'two very bad operations, one on a child'. These operations would have been undertaken under duress, without anaesthesia. It would be another twenty years before James Young Simpson, Professor of Midwifery at Edinburgh, would be the first to administer chloroform and revolutionise the practice of surgery. Luckily for Darwin, his aversion to surgical practice and medicine, in general, wasn't going to be a major problem. It was in Edinburgh that Darwin became convinced of his father's intention to provide the funds for him to live out the rest of his life in reasonable comfort. It was a belief strong enough to 'check any efforts to learn medicine'.

Darwin attended the geology and zoology lectures of Robert Jameson, which might have set the budding naturalist on an entirely different course. His recollection of the lectures was that they were 'incredibly dull' and that 'the effect they produced on me was the determination never as long as I lived to read a book on geology or in any way to study the science'.

Thomas Hope's chemistry lectures come in for only faint praise but Dr Duncan's lectures at eight o'clock on a winter's morning were 'something fearful to remember'. He found Dr Munro's lectures on human biology to be dull going and even went so far as to remark that 'the subject disgusted me'. He was later to rue the fact that he had not been encouraged to practise dissection and describes that as one of 'the greatest evils of my life'. Darwin acknowledged that the skill of dissection would have been 'invaluable for all my later work'.

Luckily, not all of Darwin's academic encounters were as stupefying. It was at Edinburgh that Darwin met the naturalist Dr Robert Grant, the first of two key figures who were to have a lasting effect on Darwin's fortunes. It was Grant who sparked Darwin's fascination with marine zoology. Charles joined the Plinian

Robert Grant.

Society and in 1826 even presented a short paper on marine animals. The nearby tidal pools along the Firth of Forth proved a happy hunting ground for the emerging naturalist and so began a lifelong fascination with the marine creatures that eke out a living between the rise and fall of the seas. It was a subject that he would come back to in earnest on his return from the *Beagle* voyage in 1836. In what might be considered a classic case of procrastination, Darwin worked on a study of molluscs on and off for the next eighteen years, only concluding his work in 1854 when he finally began work on *Origin*.

There was another encounter of note during Darwin's spell at Edinburgh. He had several lessons from John Edmonstone in the art of taxidermy. Edmonstone was a freed slave who had learned his trade from the naturalist Charles Waterton. In a letter to his sister Sarah, Darwin explained that 'I am going to learn to stuff birds, from a blackamoor I believe an old servant of Dr Duncan: it has the recommendation of cheapness, if it has nothing else, as he only charges one guinea, for an hour every day for two months.' But Darwin got much more from the experience. He would often spend time with Edmonstone who he found to be 'a very pleasant and intelligent man'. The skills he learned from Edmonstone were to be invaluable when preserving specimens during the Beagle voyage.

John Edmonstone.

7

Distractions

'My time was sadly wasted … and worse than wasted. From my passion for shooting and for hunting and when this failed for riding across country.'
Autobiography, Charles Darwin, 1876

As a young man, life for Darwin was privileged, idyllic and free from care, thanks to his father's position and wealth. Robert Darwin was greatly respected in Shrewsbury and beyond. As well as tending to the townsfolk, he had patients amongst the well-to-do families who lived in the country estates dotted about the open farmland beyond the town's boundaries. As a consequence, young Darwin's social circle included what could best be described as the children of the idle rich. Charles had begun a courtship with Fanny Owen, the sister of his school friend William who resided at Woodhouse, an impressive country house a few miles west of Shrewsbury at Rednall. In December 1828 Darwin wrote in a letter to his second cousin William Darwin Fox that 'Fanny, as all the world knows, is the prettiest, plumpest, charming personage that Shropshire possesses, ay & Birmingham too.'

They both enjoyed horse riding and Darwin stayed at Woodhouse on at least one occasion. Fanny's father, William, shared his love of country sports and enjoyed Darwin's company as she noted in a letter to her bow: 'Papa has been rather expecting you here this week to slay some of his Partridges but I suppose you have had good sport at Maer & did not return so soon as you intended.'

Summer breaks back home were devoted almost solely to leisurely pursuits, be it riding trips with his sister, strawberry picking with Fanny or shooting game at Woodhouse or Maer. Time spent at Maer Hall left him with particularly happy memories. It was the home of his uncle Josiah (Jos) Wedgwood II and as well as country sports, there were parties, lively conversation and music. Summer evenings at Maer would often find the family sitting on the steps of the portico. From there, they could see the steep, wooded bank and flower garden reflected in the lake and 'here and there a fish rising or a water-bird paddling about'.

Shooting for sport was something of a passion for Darwin. As he writes in his autobiography, 'My zeal was so great that I used to place my shooting boots open by my bed side, when I went to bed, so as not to lose half-a-minute in putting them on in the morning.'

'Uncle Jos'.

As we will learn later, Darwin would go on to study at Cambridge University where his passion for shooting would continue:

I used to practise throwing up my gun to my shoulder before a looking-glass to see that I threw it up straight. Another and a better plan was to get a friend to wave about a lighted candle, and then to fire at it with a cap on the nipple, and if the aim was accurate the little puff of air would blow out the candle. The explosion of the cap caused a sharp crack.

That sound echoed into the quad below and was misinterpreted by a passing tutor who observed, 'What an extraordinary thing it is that Mr. Darwin seems to spend hours in cracking a horsewhip in his rooms, for I often hear the crack when I pass under his windows.' Yet Darwin also felt somewhat conflicted by this 'zeal'. He persuaded himself that it was more than a sport but also 'intellectual employment', requiring 'much skill to judge where to find most game and to hunt the dogs well'.

Even when following his scientific passions, leisurely pursuits competed for his attention. His continued zeal for country sports is illustrated by an occasion when he was in Barmouth meeting friends from Cambridge. Darwin made his excuses and left for his uncle's home as 'I should have thought myself mad to give up the first days of partridge-shooting for geology or any other science.'

It was at Cambridge that Darwin made friends with a group who shared an interest in music, some of whom were musicians. Though able to appreciate it, Darwin himself had no musical abilities and confessed that he was unable to 'perceive a discord or keep time or hum a tune correctly' and considered it 'a mystery how I could possibly derive pleasure from music'.

Years later, Darwin was to marry someone musical enough for the two of them. His wife, Emma, was an accomplished pianist and her skills were put to scientific use on at least one occasion. Darwin studied the humble earthworm for the best part of forty years and was keen to discover whether they could hear. Worms were placed in pots on the piano lid and Emma was instructed to play. By this time, Darwin had already tried shouting at the worms who had also been serenaded with a bassoon and a tin whistle but the creatures had remained indifferent. With Emma at the keyboard, Darwin was able to observe the worms ducking back into their burrows, indicating that although probably deaf, they were sensitive to the vibration of the piano. It was sound, not tone that moved them.

At Cambridge, Darwin also fell in with a 'sporting set which included some dissipated, low-minded young men'. They would dine together and by Darwin's admission 'sometimes drank too much'. The meal would be followed by games of cards and 'jolly singing', though perhaps not by Darwin. He later reflected on this time with only a tinge of guilt. 'I know that I ought to feel ashamed of days and evenings thus spent, but as some of my friends were very pleasant, and we were all in the highest spirits, I cannot help looking back on these times with much pleasure.'

This love of the idle life had not gone unnoticed by Darwin's father who was becoming increasingly frustrated by his son's inability to apply himself to his academic work. But we must remember that Darwin was still in his teens and driven by the same excitement and energy that inhabits anyone of that age. Whatever he was later to become, by his admission he was not yet ready to commit to the responsibilities of adulthood. Darwin remembers his father commenting in a moment of desperation that he cared 'for nothing but shooting, dogs and rat-catching' and told him plainly that he would be a 'disgrace to himself and all his family'. The outburst was out of character for Robert and Charles retained great respect and admiration for his father describing him later as 'a remarkable man'.

Emma Wedgwood.

8

Cambridge – A Man of the Cloth?

'Considering how fiercely I have been attacked by the orthodox, it seems ludicrous that I once intended to be a clergyman.'

Autobiography, Charles Darwin, 1876

After two years at Edinburgh, it was clear to the good doctor that his son was unlikely to follow in his footsteps but he baulked at the notion that Darwin would lead the life of 'an idle sporting man'. It seemed unlikely to Robert that Darwin's interest in the natural world would offer the chance of gainful employment, so the search continued to find a suitable profession. It was common for the sons of the well-to-do to become members of parliament or officers in the army or navy. It was also considered a respectable profession to become a man of the cloth. The military would not have appealed to the family's values and their Unitarian faith may have proved problematic to any political ambition. In truth, we don't know what other options were considered but we do know that in October 1827, Darwin was directed to Cambridge to study for the clergy.

Entrance to Cambridge required a degree of competency in mathematics which Darwin did not possess, so he was first sent to a tutor in Barmouth to improve, from where he wrote to his schoolfriend Charles Whitley: 'My noddle is not capacious enough to retain or comprehend Mathematics. Beetle hunting & such things I grieve to say is my proper sphere.'

Reflecting in later life, the irony of the major proponent of the theory of evolution having previously considered the church as a profession was not lost on Darwin. But at that time, the notion of being a country clergyman perhaps held some appeal for him. Many of the clergy had embraced the current fascination with the natural world and had become keen collectors of flora and fauna. Indeed for some, like the eighteenth-century parson-naturalist Gilbert White, it was a duty to 'explore the wonders of God's creation' and at this point in his life, Darwin had not yet fully rejected the biblical account.

'It never struck me how illogical it was to say that I believed in what I could not understand and what is in fact unintelligible.' However, Darwin knew he would ultimately struggle with what he described as the 'dogmas of the Church of England'. He was to later write that,

I can indeed hardly see how anyone ought to wish Christianity to be true; for if so, the plain language of the text seems to show that men who do not

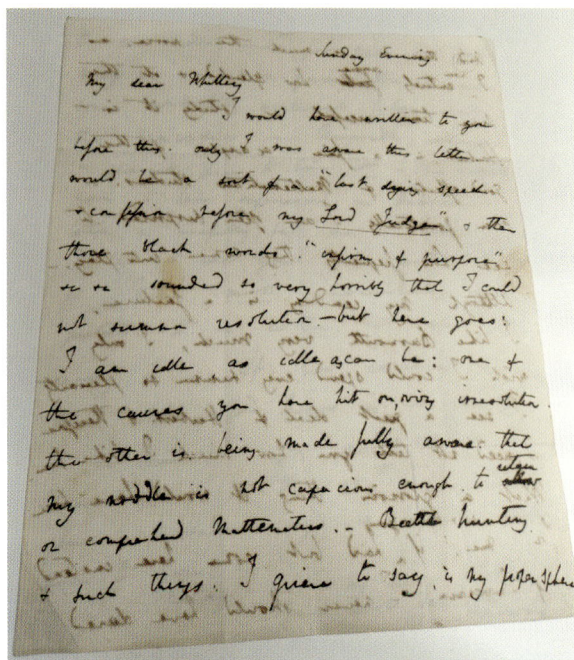

'My noddle is not capacious enough to retain or comprehend Mathematics.' (Courtesy of Shrewsbury School)

believe, and this would include my father, brother and almost all my best friends, will be everlastingly punished. And this is a damnable doctrine.

In 1831, Darwin passed his BA without distinction, but the draw of the natural sciences was now irresistible. Throughout his time at Cambridge, he continued to seek out scientific stimulation wherever he could find it. His second cousin William Darwin Fox introduced him to entomology and it fast became his latest passion. Darwin adopted the practice of collecting beetles with the same enthusiasm he had shown for marine invertebrates whilst in Edinburgh. On one occasion he took his pastime to extremes:

I saw two rare beetles and seized one in each hand; then I saw a third and new kind, which I could not bear to lose, so that I popped the one which I held in my right hand into my mouth. Alas, it ejected some intensely acrid fluid, which burnt my tongue so that I was forced to spit the beetle out, which was lost.

It was in Cambridge that Darwin encountered John Stevens Henslow, a priest and scientist and the second key figure after Grant to have a profound influence on Darwin's scientific trajectory. Darwin was already aware of Henslow's reputation as both his brother and cousin held him in high regard. Ras had described Henslow as 'a man who knew every branch of science' while Fox viewed Henslow as 'a clever and most pleasant man'. Henslow kept open house once every week and through Fox, Darwin became one of the regulars. He was impressed by

Henslow's breadth of knowledge being 'great in botany, entomology, chemistry, minerology and geology'. The young man spent more and more time in Henslow's company and was often invited to join the family for dinner. Other dons had noticed this close relationship and referred to Darwin as 'the man who walks with Henslow'. Henslow introduced Darwin to his wider circle of friends. Though not all academics, they were all of a greater age which caused Darwin to later reflect: 'Looking back, I infer that there must have been something in me a little superior to the common run of youths otherwise, those so much older than me and higher in academic position, would never have allowed me to associate with them.'

It was Henslow who encouraged Darwin to look to geology as an area of science on which to apply his considerable enthusiasm and despite his bad experiences at Edinburgh University, he now embraced it. Back in Shropshire he 'examined sections and coloured a map of parts around Shrewsbury'. He joined the geology professor Adam Sedgwick on his annual field trip to Wales, a landscape familiar to him from his many family trips to the area as a child and his own more recent entomological sorties.

In contrast to Darwin's theological scepticism, Henslow was devout but a shared interest in the natural world made them firm friends. Henslow saw promise in Darwin and a genuine willingness to learn. Of all the associations Darwin developed amongst the scientific community, it was arguably the relationship with Henslow that was the most significant. As Darwin himself said, 'it influenced my career more than any other'.

One public school and two universities later, Darwin's summation of his formal education was blunt: 'During the three years which I spent at Cambridge my time was wasted, as far as academical studies were concerned, as completely as at Edinburgh and at school.'

John Stevens Henslow.

9

The Letter

'Don't put on any modest doubts or fears about your disqualifications for I assure you I think you are the very man they are in search of.'
Henslow writing to Darwin, 24 August 1831

With Darwin distracted from his theological studies by leisurely pursuits and the lure of the natural world, it would not be a great leap of the imagination to suggest that the atmosphere at the family home was becoming tense, at least in respect of Darwin's prospects and his father's ambitions for them. By now, it would have been clear to Robert that his son had set his mind on a particular course and that his efforts to reign him in were failing.

During his time at Cambridge, Darwin had been quite taken by the writings of Herschel and Humboldt and in particular, the latter's notes on Tenerife as they appeared in his *Personal Narrative*. So inspired was Darwin by the naturalist's description that he began to plan a voyage there. He managed to get an introduction to a merchant in London to make enquiries about a ship. But his plans were to be overtaken by a far more exciting opportunity that was just around the corner.

On the southern tip of South America, the coastline is fractured and fragmented. Part of this wind-swept, desolate land is called Tierra Del Fuego, or 'Land of Fire'. Nearby, at Cape Horn, the Pacific, Southern and Atlantic oceans meet creating a stormy cauldron that has become the graveyard for many an unfortunate mariner over the centuries.

While Darwin was studying in England, a British naval vessel, HMS *Beagle*, under the command of Captain Robert Fitzroy was sailing these unsettled seas and attempting to improve on the existing coastal charts. While the ship pitched and rolled in the foamy brine, Fitzroy dreamt of a great adventure, a circumnavigation of the globe. Though he would not be the first to achieve the feat he would ensure that the voyage had merit. He would take a naturalist who would bring scientific rigour to the venture. He would need support from the admiralty and he would need to recruit the right person for the position of naturalist. So, as the *Beagle* bobbed about in the choppy waters off South America and with sextant in hand, Fitzroy pondered how to make his dream a reality.

Fitzroy made contact with the Hydrographer of the Royal Navy, Captain Francis Beaufort, to discuss his plan. The two had much in common. They shared a perhaps unsurprising interest in the weather. Beaufort had recently devised the empirical measure or scale of wind speed that is used to this day but was to be first deployed during the forthcoming voyage of the *Beagle*. Fitzroy was pondering whether it would be possible to find a means of predicting the weather, for such a system would surely save the lives of many a seafarer. He was later to establish a chain of observation posts and a means by which to collate the data they gathered. Weather patterns could then be recorded and issued in the form of bulletins. His work would culminate in the founding of the Meteorological Office; Fitzroy was the first weatherman.

Robert Fitzroy, captain of HMS *Beagle*.

Francis Beaufort.

Fitzroy explained to his friend the scope of his adventure and the proposition 'that some well-educated and scientific person should be sought for who would willingly share such accommodation as I had to offer, in order to profit by the opportunity of visiting distant countries yet little known'. Beaufort offered to help by contacting an acquaintance of his, George Peacock of Trinity College, Cambridge, to see if he could recommend a 'proper person to go out as a naturalist'. Peacock had two names in mind: Henslow and Henslow's brother-in-law, the Revd Leonard Jenyns, Vicar of Swaffham Bulbeck. Jenyns was a keen naturalist and certainly had all the attributes Fitzroy was looking for. Peacock wrote to Henslow in August 1831 and also approached the good vicar with the proposition, but both declined; Henslow cited family responsibilities and Jenyns, parish commitments. Both men agreed, however, that there was someone who 'in all respects, would be a fit man to go', a young man whose dedication to the natural sciences they had come to admire.

When Darwin returned home from his Welsh field trip with Sedgwick, a letter from Henslow was waiting. Although its route had been tortuous, the offer of adventure had finally arrived in Shrewsbury. Reading *Wonders of the World* in his early schooldays had infected Darwin with a 'wish to travel to remote countries'. As we know, Darwin had already made enquiries in London to find a ship of his own to sail to Tenerife but here was a promise of a far more ambitious voyage. As if to excite Darwin even more, Henslow wrote in the letter that 'there never was a finer chance for a man of zeal & spirit'.

Perspective is a key factor in our story of Darwin and the development of his great idea, but at this point in the narrative conflicting perspectives threaten to derail the course of history. Henslow and Sedgwick were among many who, during his studies in Edinburgh and Cambridge had seen in Darwin a bright, thoughtful and diligent young student. By contrast, Robert Darwin had seen in his son a reckless youth, unable to apply himself seriously to the study of first medicine and then theology. He saw a smart boy too easily distracted by social and sporting pursuits who had so far failed to display a willingness to settle in any profession.

One can imagine Darwin felt a slight sense of trepidation as he handed the letter to his father for without Robert's permission any dream of adventure was dead in the water. To Darwin's horror, on reading the letter, Robert described the proposition as 'a useless undertaking' that would divert him from his career path into the clergy. Darwin could see his chance of a lifetime being snatched from his hands. There was, however, one caveat. Robert told his son: 'if you can find any man of common sense, who advises you to go, I will give my consent'. Instead of responding to Fitzroy's offer with enthusiasm, Darwin was thrown into an unfortunate impasse. On 30 August, with a heavy heart, Darwin wrote back to Henslow respectfully declining the offer that had come from Fitzroy via Beaufort and Peacock. He explained:

> As far as my own mind is concerned, I should I think, certainly most gladly have accepted the opportunity, which you so kindly have offered me. – But my Father, although he does not decidedly refuse me, gives such strong advice against going. – that I should not be comfortable, if I did not follow it.

However, there was a man of 'common sense' that Darwin had in mind. Over the years, he had become extremely fond of his Uncle Jos. The summers spent at Maer

Hall had been idyllic and nephew and uncle were firm friends, so Darwin decided to go to Maer at the first opportunity and ask his uncle to intercede on his behalf. It was the intervention of Wedgwood that eventually changed Robert's mind. Perhaps Wedgwood's perspective on Darwin's character surprised the doctor. It would certainly have been closer to that of Henslow. If perhaps not enthusiastic, Robert agreed that there may be some merit in the experience. If nothing else, it would certainly make the content of the Reverend Darwin's sermons more colourful when he finally settled down in a parish.

As father and son discussed the details, it became clear that the position was as a gentleman naturalist and came with no salary from the Admiralty. Not for the first time, Darwin would be reliant on an allowance from his father. He admitted to being rather extravagant at Cambridge and needed to reassure his father that he would be more fiscally responsible this time. Darwin argued that being at sea for long periods meant he would be 'deuced clever to spend more than my allowance whilst on board the Beagle', to which his father replied 'but they all tell me you are very clever'.

His father had finally said yes, but Darwin had written to Henslow declining the offer. Henslow had written to Darwin on 24 August but Darwin hadn't had sight of the offer letter until he returned from Wales on the 29th and then there were the tortuous negotiations with his father. The delay may have scuppered any chance of Darwin taking the position. For all he knew, Captain Fitzroy may have found someone else to act as companion and collector. On 1 September, Darwin wrote to Beaufort and held his breath:

> Perhaps you may have received a letter from Mr. Peacock, stating my refusal; this was owing to my Father not at first approving of the plan, since which time he has reconsidered the subject: & has given his consent & therefore if the appointment is not already filled up, – I shall be very happy to have the honor of accepting it.

With no telegraph, the mail coach was still the fastest way to communicate over distance, so Darwin's letter would have made its way across town to the Lion Hotel at the top of the street called Wyle Cop to begin its long journey, accompanied no doubt by Darwin's sincere hopes for a positive outcome.

As the shortlist of candidates became shorter, Darwin's chances were improving but he was by no means a shoo-in for the position. When they finally met, Fitzroy harboured doubts about the young Darwin's suitability for the job. The captain was influenced by Lavater's theories on physiognomy, a pseudo-science that held great store in judging a person's character by the shape of their head and facial features. Based on the shape of Darwin's nose, Fitzroy was not entirely convinced that he could 'possess sufficient energy and determination for the voyage'. He needn't have had such doubts. By now, Darwin was by any measure the right man for the job.

Matters developed at pace from this point as a letter from Fanny Owen illustrates:

'My Dear Charles, I have this evening heard from Caroline that you leave home the end of this week—and that you wish to have a good bye from me before you go. I had not the least idea you were to go so soon.' She went on to wish him well in his adventure, albeit with a tinge of sadness: 'I do hope you will enjoy yourself & be the happiest of the happy, I would give anything to see you once more before you go, for it does make me melancholy to think the time you are to be away.'

Despite the tenderness and affection illustrated in their letters, the romance did not survive the voyage and Fanny later married Robert Myddelton Biddulph of Chirk Castle, a grand property and estate across the Welsh border.

10

A Head for Adventure

'One whole night I tried to think over the pleasure of seeing Shrewsbury again, but the barren plains of Peru gained the day.'

Darwin writing to his sister Catherine from Valparaiso, 8 November 1834

HMS *Beagle* sailed from Devonport on 27 December 1831. The original plan was to make land at Tenerife but they were refused anchor for fear that the crew may have brought cholera to the local population. Captain Fitzroy left the Canaries and charted a course to Cape Verde. On 16 January 1832, Darwin finally stepped off the *Beagle* at Porto Praya and with a volume of Lyell's *Principles of Geology* in hand the twenty-two-year-old strode out to explore the landscape with a bravado that only youth can muster. At this point, Darwin couldn't imagine the variety of flora and fauna he would encounter during the five years of the voyage but he would be ready, notebook in hand, to record everything he possibly could. Darwin was young, ambitious and for perhaps the first time in his life, focused. However much Darwin may have been distracted in his student years, he was now paying attention. His great adventure had begun in earnest.

Ostensibly a sea voyage, the young naturalist had many opportunities to explore the interior of the countries on the itinerary. When the *Beagle* dropped anchor, Darwin would disembark and set off on his explorations to be picked up later at an agreed place and time. In this way, he spent a great deal of the five years of the voyage on land. Darwin recalls in his famous account that the main object of the voyage was to, 'Complete the survey of Patagonia and Tierra Del Fuego… to survey the shores of Chile, Peru, and some of the islands in the Pacific … and to carry out a chain of chronometrical measurements round the world.'

Darwin was impressed by Captain Fitzroy and described him as 'devoted to his duty, generous to a fault' and 'an ardent friend to all under his sway'. It's just as well that they did hit it off, for the two men were to share a cabin for the duration of the voyage. One aspect of Fitzroy's character was not so winning: his temper. Officers changing watch would enquire of their colleague 'whether much hot coffee had been served up this morning?' alluding to the captain's sometimes short fuse. Indeed Darwin and Fitzroy fell into arguments on a few occasions. One incident in particular took place when the *Beagle* was moored off the Brazilian coast. Fitzroy had returned from a visit to a plantation and spoke in defence of the practice of slavery saying that the owner had gathered a number of

Darwin in his twenties, sketch by G. Richmond.

his workers together and asked them in Fitzroy's presence whether any of them wished to be free, to which they had replied 'no'. Darwin was not impressed with Fitzroy's account and asked 'with a sneer, whether he thought that the answers of slaves in the presence of their master was worth anything'. Darwin's response is perhaps not surprising considering how ardent an abolitionist Josiah Wedgwood, his maternal grandfather, was. On another occasion, the two had fallen out over the matter of a reception Fitzroy had been duty-bound to host. After the minor spat, Darwin left the ship and on his return equilibrium had been restored. The first lieutenant, however, took Darwin aside to remonstrate with him saying, 'Confound you, philosopher, I wish you would not quarrel with the skipper; the day you left the ship … he kept me walking the deck till midnight, abusing you all the time.' Their relationship fared poorly when the voyage was over and Darwin met Fitzroy only occasionally as he was 'always afraid of unintentionally offending him' and did so once 'almost beyond mutual reconciliation'. The matter that drove them irrevocably apart was the publication of *Origin* with Fitzroy expressing his indignation for Darwin having published 'so unorthodox a book'.

It was during the *Beagle* voyage that Darwin's youthful passion for shooting game diminished. In the first two years, he was as enthusiastic as he had ever been but he confesses, 'I gave up my gun more and more, and finally altogether … as shooting interfered with my work.' He had come to realise that 'the pleasure of observing and reasoning was a much higher one than that of skill and sport'. Darwin went further to reflect that 'the primeval instincts of the barbarian slowly yielded to the acquired tastes of the civilised man'.

In 1835, the fourth year of the voyage, the *Beagle* reached the Galapagos Islands. On the 17 September, they landed on Chatham Island and Darwin's first impression was one of disappointment: 'nothing could be less inviting than the first appearance'. He went on to describe 'a broken field of black basaltic lava' covered everywhere 'by stunted, sun-burnt brushwood, which shows little signs of life'. Pickings were slim on Chatham Island for the young naturalist who 'diligently tried to collect as many plants as possible' but 'succeeded in getting very few'. This island chain 'formed by volcanic rocks' would have appeared almost alien yet in its innumerable craters Darwin was reminded of the scarred landscape of Staffordshire 'where the great iron-foundries are most numerous'. Darwin was struck by the 'singular relations of the animals and plants inhabiting several islands of the Galapagos archipelago' to those he had observed in South America. There appeared to be quirks of nature on these remote and individually distinctive islands that he hadn't observed on the mainland or at least not to the same extent. Finches that at first sight appeared to be of the same species had, on closer inspection, slight or sometimes striking differences in the shape of their beaks. The now-famous giant tortoises displayed even more dramatic variations in the shape of their shells from island to island. Darwin was bright enough to consider that there were forces at play here but not so smart that he could explain what they were, at least not yet. If he had come to that startling realisation on the remote archipelago there would be some written record, bearing in mind the copious contemporaneous notes that survive. But every indication is that the hypothesis slowly dawned on him as he reflected on his notes after his return. Ultimately, it was his observation of adaptation by these species that was to form the foundation of his great work but *Origin* was many years off. For now, he would observe, collect and record. Darwin was making scientific notes, sending home specimens, corresponding with his family in Shrewsbury and keeping a diary of the voyage. Day-to-day occurrences were easy enough to record but he confessed in a letter to his sister Caroline that he grappled with the process of putting his scientific notes down on paper:

'Where reasoning comes into play, to make a proper connection, a clearness & a moderate fluency, is to me, as I have said, a difficulty of which I had no idea.' It's a startling confession considering the apparent ease with which he later expressed his great idea in the pages of *Origin*. Darwin is most often viewed as the assured elder statesman of science which he undoubtedly became, but here is a young man of twenty-seven relishing his opportunity to observe so much yet struggling to convey his thoughts on the significance of what he was seeing. During the voyage, he showed his diary to Fitzroy who remarked that it may be worth publishing, an astute observation as Darwin's *The Voyage of The Beagle*, published in 1839, was an instant success.

Darwin was aware of the opportunity the voyage had given him and that it had provided 'the first real training or education of my mind. I was led to attend closely to several branches of natural history, and thus my powers of observation were improved, though they were already fairly developed'.

Whilst on Ascension Island in the last stages of the voyage Darwin learned that Adam Sedgwick had called on his father in Shrewsbury to suggest that his son 'should take a place amongst the leading scientific men'. The news was welcome if a little puzzling as Darwin could not understand how Sedgwick could have 'learnt anything of my proceedings'.

Darwin had been in regular contact with Henslow and surmised that it was he who had probably shared some of his letters with the Philosophical Society of Cambridge which alerted Sedgwick to the significance of the work he had been undertaking. When HMS *Beagle* docked at Falmouth on 2 October 1836, Darwin had transformed from a keen young enthusiast to a fully-fledged Man of Science.

Darwin hadn't attended Edinburgh or Cambridge to gain formal training in the natural sciences; he'd sought out lectures on the subject in an extracurricular fashion. Through his enthusiasm, Darwin had acquired sufficient skills to fulfil his duties on the *Beagle*. At university Darwin's mentors, Grant, Henslow and Sedgwick, would have instilled in their protege the need to record his observations but this was a discipline already familiar to him; it was something he would have been made aware of in childhood back at the family home in Shrewsbury. As we've learned, the family kept detailed records of planting and progress in a set of perennial garden diaries. From an early age, Darwin was shown the benefits of observing and recording. Combined with the chemistry experiments he conducted with his brother Erasmus in an outbuilding at The Mount, these were skills that would serve him well not just on the *Beagle* voyage but throughout his life. It is also interesting to note that Darwin's garden at his house in Kent became, in effect, his laboratory, reflecting his childhood experiences in Shrewsbury. With the vital skills of observing and recording taught at such an early age, the Darwin family's garden diaries are the third and final pillar.

11

Goodbye to Shrewsbury

'The Beagle arrived at Falmouth on Sunday evening, & I reached home late last night. My head is quite confused with so much delight, but I cannot allow my sisters to tell you first, how happy I am to see all my dear friends again.'

Darwin writing to Uncle Jos, 5 October 1836

The long coach ride home had offered time for reflection and Darwin observed that 'all England appears changed, excepting the good old Town of Shrewsbury & its inhabitants – which for all I can see to the contrary may go on as they now are to Doomsday'.

Yet, in all his excitement, Darwin had not forgotten how much he owed Uncle Jos for securing his father's permission to join the *Beagle*, writing in his letter of 5 October, 'I hope in person to thank you, as being my first Lord of the Admiralty.' Adding, breathlessly, 'I am so very happy I hardly know what I am writing.'

When Darwin returned to his family home he 'found all my dear good sisters & father quite well – My father appears more cheerful and very little older than when I left. My sisters assure me I do not look the least different, & I am able to return the compliment'.

It seems his father did not share the view of Darwin's sisters. Images that survive of Darwin as a young man clearly show that his hairline was receding, which may have caused his father to comment, 'Why, the shape of his head is quite altered.'

Darwin's stay in Shrewsbury was to be brief; there was work to be done. The letters and specimens he had been sending back to England throughout his voyage on the *Beagle* had made quite an impression. Having circumnavigated the globe, he could now set aside any thoughts of joining the clergy and chart a course into the scientific world. Darwin would now follow Sedgwick's advice and take his place 'amongst the leading scientific men'. He finally bade farewell to his beloved Shrewsbury and took lodgings in Cambridge to start the exhaustive work of cataloguing his collection and to begin writing up an account of his adventure.

There were other considerations as Darwin confided to his old schoolfriend Whitley:

'As for a wife, that most interesting specimen in the whole series of vertebrate animals, Providence only know whether I shall ever capture one or even be able to feed her if caught.'

Fanny Owen was now married and settled in Chirk Castle and Darwin began a romantic association with his cousin Emma Wedgwood, the daughter of his beloved Uncle Jos. The two would have moved in the same social circles since childhood but now they were courting. The relationship was soon to be formalised as Darwin wrote in a letter to Whitley, 'I am going to be married. The lady in question is my cousin Miss Emma Wedgwood – you will approve of marrying cousins.' Whitley had indeed also married his cousin.

A letter written by Emma to Charles on 23 January 1839 reveals a charming aspect of their partnership as Emma teases Darwin for being too analytical: 'I believe from your account of your own mind that you will only consider me as

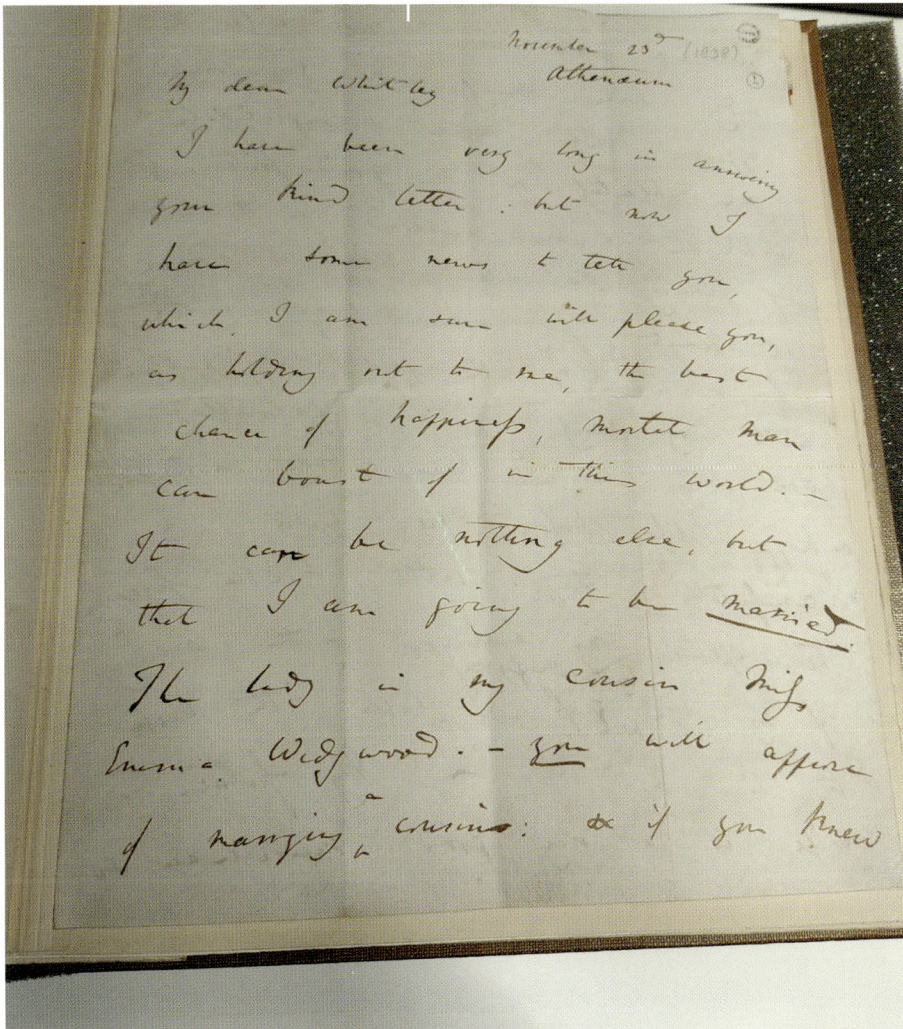

'I am going to be married.' (Courtesy of Shrewsbury School)

a specimen of the genus (I don't know what simia I believe). You will be forming theories about me & if I am cross or out of temper you will only consider "What does that prove".'

Emma can be forgiven for making such an observation when you consider that shortly after she had accepted his proposal of marriage the year before, Darwin had made a somewhat clinical list of the pros and cons of getting wed and had included on the benefits side: 'Constant companion, (& friend in old age) who will feel interested in one,— object to be beloved & played with.— —better than a dog anyhow.'

Emma's letter of the 23rd also gives us a clear indication that there was at least one topic on which they disagreed. 'I do hope that though our opinions may not agree upon all points of religion we may sympathize a good deal in our feelings on the subject.'

A week later, Charles and Emma married at St Peter's Church, Maer, a short walk from her family home. Within three years they had found a place to settle, a fine house with gardens in the village of Downe in Kent. His garden became his laboratory, his young children his willing assistants. At Down House, he charmed worms, studied carnivorous plants, wrote, walked, and though dogged by ill health, enjoyed the happiest of marriages. Darwin was now ruminating on his big idea and the impact it was likely to have not just on the world at large but closer to home. Emma had a strong faith and Darwin's train of thought was moving in a very different direction. Some fifteen years before the publication of his work he describes in a letter to his great friend the botanist Joseph Hooker that the revelation of his idea was akin to 'confessing to a murder'. But through it all, Emma supported and loved him as he loved her.

Darwin planned to lay out his great idea in a 'big book', three mighty tomes on which he would spend the next few years working before finally sending them for publication. Now fully settled at Down House, he had his family, his home comforts, his study and a close group of friends who would visit from time to time.

Darwin's days of adventure and long field trips were over. He was now in almost permanent residence at Down House. He began the practice of prolific correspondence with naturalists and collectors around the world. This process of sharing information to amass knowledge could be seen as an early form of crowdsourcing and it was the frequency and efficiency of the mail service in Darwin's day that made this possible.

Life was good but Darwin's well-laid plan was about to go awry. Unbeknown to him, someone else had been ruminating on the diversity of life, chiefly as a consequence of the fauna encountered on voyages around the Spice Islands, or north-eastern Indonesia as we now know the region today. Alfred Russel Wallace had been making a meagre living sending back specimens of exotic wildlife to a clientele of eager amateur naturalists back home in England. He was asking himself what could account for the changes that he observed in creatures that on

Maer Hall viewed from St Peter's churchyard.

the face of it were related and yet had somehow undergone subtle changes from island to island?

He gathered his thoughts and committed his conclusions to paper. Who then, he asked himself, should he send his idea to? Who would take it seriously or at the very least cast a friendly, critical eye over it? Why not the author of the best-selling *The Voyage of the Beagle*? Here was someone who knew what it was like to travel the world and encounter the wonders of nature. And so it was that a parcel arrived at Down House. Darwin read the covering letter signed by Wallace and then proceeded to consume the contents of the enclosed essay. With perhaps a growing sense of

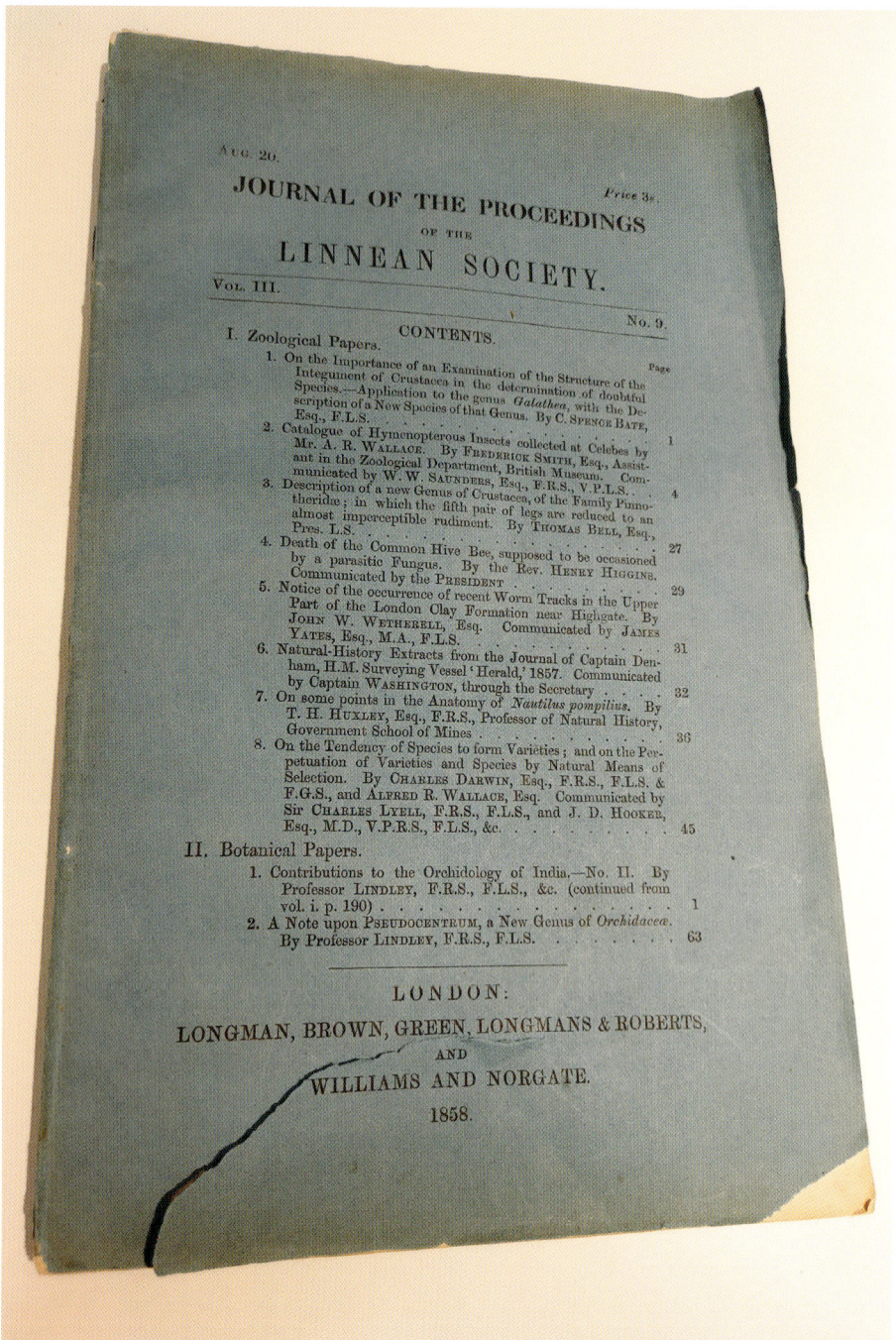

Aug. 20.

JOURNAL OF THE PROCEEDINGS
OF THE
LINNEAN SOCIETY.

Price 3s.

VOL. III.

No. 9.

CONTENTS.

I. Zoological Papers.

Page

1. On the Importance of an Examination of the Structure of the Integument of Crustacea in the determination of doubtful Species.—Application to the genus *Galathea*, with the Description of a New Species of that Genus. By C. SPENCE BATE, Esq., F.L.S. 1

2. Catalogue of Hymenopterous Insects collected at Celebes by Mr. A. R. WALLACE. By FREDERICK SMITH, Esq., Assistant in the Zoological Department, British Museum. Communicated by W. W. SAUNDERS, Esq., F.R.S., V.P.L.S. . . 4

3. Description of a new Genus of Crustacea, of the Family Pinnotheridæ; in which the fifth pair of legs are reduced to an almost imperceptible rudiment. By THOMAS BELL, Esq., Pres. L.S. 27

4. Death of the Common Hive Bee, supposed to be occasioned by a parasitic Fungus. By the Rev. HENRY HIGGINS. Communicated by the PRESIDENT 29

5. Notice of the occurrence of recent Worm Tracks in the Upper Part of the London Clay Formation near Highgate. By JOHN W. WETHERELL, Esq. Communicated by JAMES YATES, Esq., M.A., F.L.S. 31

6. Natural-History Extracts from the Journal of Captain Denham, H.M. Surveying Vessel 'Herald,' 1857. Communicated by Captain WASHINGTON, through the Secretary 32

7. On some points in the Anatomy of *Nautilus pompilius*. By T. H. HUXLEY, Esq., F.R.S., Professor of Natural History, Government School of Mines 36

8. On the Tendency of Species to form Varieties; and on the Perpetuation of Varieties and Species by Natural Means of Selection. By CHARLES DARWIN, Esq., F.R.S., F.L.S. & F.G.S., and ALFRED R. WALLACE, Esq. Communicated by Sir CHARLES LYELL, F.R.S., F.L.S., and J. D. HOOKER, Esq., M.D., V.P.R.S., F.L.S., &c. 45

II. Botanical Papers.

1. Contributions to the Orchidology of India.—No. II. By Professor LINDLEY, F.R.S., F.L.S., &c. (continued from vol. i. p. 190) 1

2. A Note upon PSEUDOCENTRUM, a New Genus of *Orchidaceæ*. By Professor LINDLEY, F.R.S., F.L.S. 63

LONDON:

LONGMAN, BROWN, GREEN, LONGMANS & ROBERTS,

AND

WILLIAMS AND NORGATE.

1858.

Linnean Society Proceedings, Zoological Papers, Item 8: 'On the Tendency of Species by Natural Means of Selection', By Charles Darwin and Alfred R. Wallace.

disbelief, Darwin saw his own idea staring back at him from the pages of Wallace's work. In a letter to his friend Charles Lyell he wrote, 'I never saw a more striking coincidence ... all my originality, whatever it may amount to, will be smashed.'

What to do? The advice from Lyell and his other great friend Hooker was to go to print at once. Wallace could not be ignored nor his work be dismissed, so a compromise was reached. The works would be given equal credit. At a meeting of the Linnaean Society on 1 July 1858, a hastily drafted paper from Darwin and the one from Wallace were presented by Lyell and Hooker. Neither Wallace nor Darwin was present, Charles still grieving the loss of his son, also called Charles, just four days earlier from scarlet fever.

Afterwards, Darwin rushed into print with a shorter and as a consequence more digestible version of his ideas. *On the Origin of Species by Means of Natural Selection, or the Preservation of Favoured Races in the Struggle for Life* was published by John Murray of London on 24 November 1859. Like his memoir of the *Beagle* voyage, *Origin* became an instant bestseller.

Above left: Joseph Dalton Hooker.

Above right: Alfred Russel Wallace.

12

What's the Big Idea?

'I will here give a brief sketch of the progress of opinion on the Origin of Species. Until recently the great majority of naturalists believed that species were immutable productions, and had been separately created.'

Origin of Species, Charles Darwin, 1859

Darwin's great idea was received warmly in most scientific circles and not so warmly in others. Although the process of evolution has become woven into the practice of any number of scientific fields, not least in our ability to develop vaccines through an understanding of how a virus can adapt, there continue to be those who are unable to accept the theory of evolution because they adhere to the notion of creation. Some see the complexity of life as the intricate workings of a

Darwin *c.* 1854.

clock, the construction of which requires a watchmaker and not the consequence of the chain of happy accidents that Darwin proposed.

Darwin's work on the origin of species is sometimes dismissed by those naysayers as only a theory. But the term 'theory' in a scientific context should not be confused with the word when it's used to describe a simple hunch. If one wants to put forward a scientific proposition the process is rigorous. It must stand up to scrutiny from scientific peers and then and only then does it become accepted as a theory.

So what is this idea sparked by observations during a great voyage, so thoughtfully fermented for years yet hurriedly rushed into print by circumstances beyond Darwin's control, that caused a seismic shift in our understanding of the development of life on Earth? How did it challenge the status quo and what was the context?

Speculation on the matter of how species come into being had been going on for some time. Erasmus Darwin had entered the field two generations before Charles in his work *Zoonomia*. As we know, Darwin enjoyed his grandfather's work during his years at university but after time had come to feel that it had little in the form of substance. It was, Darwin believed, an opinion without evidence and could not be elevated above speculation. He was of the firm belief that ideas or propositions need evidence to support them. The actions of the laws described by Darwin in *Origin* are observable, recordable and repeatable.

Erasmus had leaned in the direction of the French naturalist Jean-Baptiste Lamarck. Darwin too shared Lamarck's belief in the importance of adaptation but the two differed in their understanding of when, why and how adaptation occurred. Lamarck had a view that change happened within a generation. The classic example is a four-legged, horse-like animal that strains to stretch its neck to reach higher into the trees where the source of food is plentiful. This creature's progeny would then inherit a slightly longer neck and if the practice is repeated through enough generations, you end up with a giraffe.

But Darwin couldn't accept that change occurred as Lamarck described it. For one thing, if an acquired variance is inherited, surely the son of someone who lost a digit in an accident would be born with nine fingers, an oversimplification, granted, but you can see where Lamarck's reasoning starts to falter under examination. Lamarck also believed in orthogenesis, the notion that life is climbing up a 'ladder of progress' becoming more complex over time. And while it is true that we have evolved from more primitive hominids, some of our ancestors remain in the trees. A popular creationist criticism is that if we are descended from apes, why do we still have monkeys? But reflect for a moment on the extent to which complex marine life in our oceans is dependent on the simple, minute drifters or wanderers we call plankton for their major food source. Complexity lives alongside simplicity and often the two are interdependent. It's a phenomenon that Darwin was able to illustrate in a simple doodle he produced in his study at Down House.

Darwin's sketch resembles a tree with several branches, so let's continue the arboreal analogy, let's imagine fruit at the end of each branch which represents all

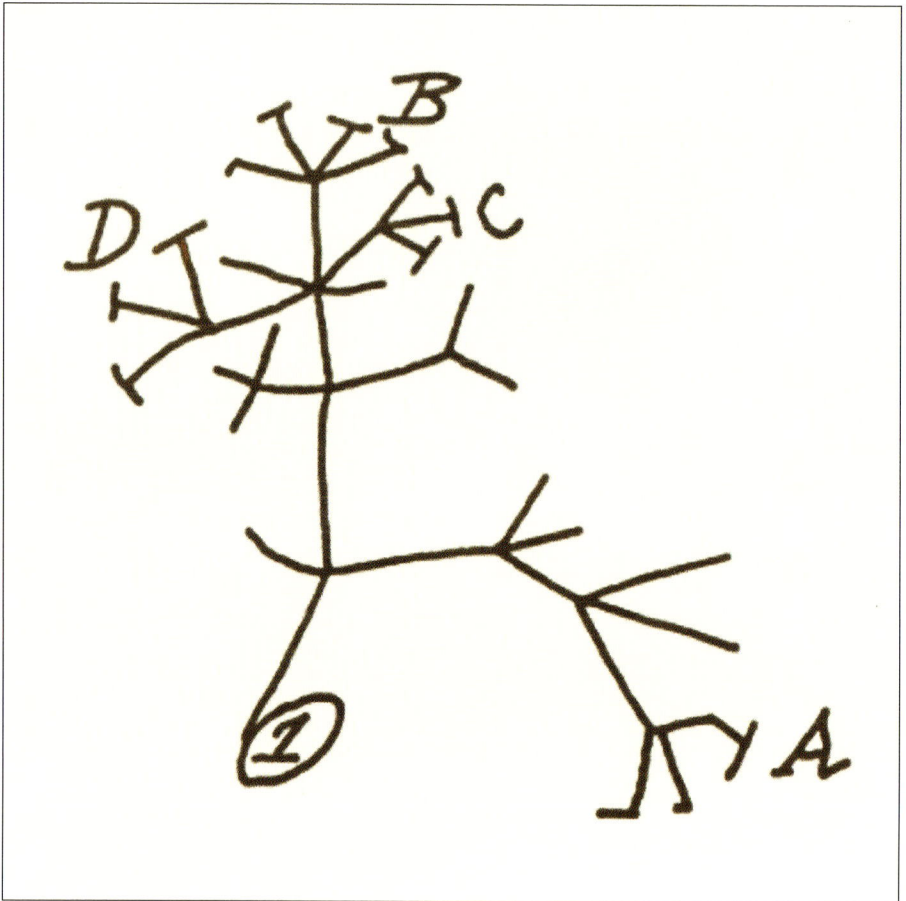

Darwin's sketch of his tree of evolution.

of the species present on our planet. Some fruit will thrive and ripen and some will wither before their seeds can be sown and germinate. Darwin argued that natural laws had created variety as a consequence of changes brought about by the power of circumstance. The circumstances are partly environmental such as changes in climate, or scarcity of food. But they were also biological, one subject's immunity to disease or infection allowing it to survive when others of its species perished. They were adaptations necessary for survival.

Darwin understood that life does not exist in a fixed state, change is constant and the ability to adapt places a creature in a better position to pass on its traits to the next generation through reproduction. Significantly, Darwin believed that the subtle differences within a given species in a given generation are purely accidental. They are freaks of nature not deliberate or designed. However, if they prove advantageous, these traits can persist through generations, becoming magnified until a new species is created.

Species are specialists, some more so than others. Going back through the notes he had made whilst on the Galapagos, Darwin reflected on the differing shapes of beaks on the finches and the variety of shapes of the shells of the giant tortoise as they contrasted from island to island. Darwin deduced that each species was perfectly adapted to reach the food source that sustained it in that specific location.

Adaptation is the key and an extreme example would be the giant anteater which has evolved to become, in effect, an ant-eating machine. Over time, its proboscis has become elongated and tapered and its tongue long and probing. In its predation and consumption of ants and termites, the anteater has few competitors but give it a cheese sandwich to eat and it doesn't look so smart. Chimpanzees, on the other hand, have learned to use tools in the form of twigs to reach into termite mounds and fish for ants. In comparing the anteater and the chimpanzee we can see that evolution throws up some novel solutions but they aren't always sustainable ones.

Humans, like chimpanzees, are omnivores which gives us something of an advantage. In our early history, we were nomadic hunter-gatherers, going where the food was. We later settled and became farmers and grew the food we needed. And, like chimpanzees, we are also problem-solvers using our wits to adapt rather than rely on tiny, incremental changes over millennia. Look at our technological progress in a few centuries and compare the appearance of modern man with our homo sapien ancestor who evolved from its primitive hominid contemporaries between 200,000 and 300,00 years ago and we differ little. What has evolved and grown considerably is our brain, our intellectual capacity and our imagination. Life is fragile and a change of circumstance, however apparently small, can have catastrophic consequences for species that can't adapt. The fallout from the Industrial Revolution and the explosion of the human population have accounted for the loss of species at an alarming rate. We have changed the circumstances for life on Earth within a few generations and the consequences for nature are irrevocable.

And so we learn that Darwin was not referring to the survival of the fittest but survival by those who are most fit to survive and reproduce in a given circumstance. Great dinosaurs once ruled the world but when a huge meteor struck what we now call the Gulf of Mexico causing a global climactic disaster, no amount of sharp teeth, horns or bulk was enough to avoid extinction. It was far more advantageous to be a small, furry mammal.

Again, it is worth underlining that Darwin reached his conclusion at a time when, as he admitted, 'the laws governing inheritance are quite unknown'. After Darwin's death, the work of Gregor Mendel began to reach a wider audience. We now know that the mechanism for the transference of these advantageous traits is genetic material passed from one generation to another. Genetics was a great leap forward in our scientific understanding but it only served to underpin Darwin's theory.

When one reflects on the fragility of life and those who have perished throughout history by natural disaster, war, plague, pestilence or extinction, is it not humbling to reflect that because of the ability to adapt, even though so many living things have perished, you and I and every living thing presently on this planet is directly tied by an unbroken thread to the first spark of life on Earth?

As we have heard, *On the Origin of Species* was not the 'big book' that Darwin planned to write. The paper sent by Wallace hurried Darwin into print. Yet the result of all that haste was a work of not just brevity but clarity. Did this account for its popularity? It was certainly into its second edition within a year of publication and has never been out of print. Having watched his good friend labour for more than twenty years on his magnum opus, Joseph Hooker now felt able to express his honest opinion in a letter to Darwin. 'I am all the more glad that you have published in this form, for the three volumes, unprefaced by this, would have choked any naturalist of the nineteenth century.'

In 1894, in a speech to the Royal Society, Darwin's other great friend Thomas Huxley said:

'I am as much convinced now as I was 34 years ago that the theory propounded by Mr. Darwin ... has never yet been shown to be inconsistent with any positive observations ... I do believe that on all grounds of pure science it "holds the ground".'

Thomas Huxley.

Each year, at the annual birthday toast it is traditional to read an extract from the conclusion of *Origin*. The language is clear with even a hint of romanticism and as a summary of his great idea, it is hard to improve on. Here is that extract, you can judge for yourself:

> It is interesting to contemplate an entangled bank, clothed with many plants of many kinds, with birds singing on the bushes, with various insects flitting about, and with worms crawling through the damp earth, and to reflect that these elaborately constructed forms, so different from each other, and dependent on each other in so complex a manner, have all been produced by laws acting around us … There is grandeur in this view of life, with its several powers, having been originally breathed into a few forms or into one; and that, whilst this planet has gone cycling on according to the fixed law of gravity, from so simple a beginning endless forms most beautiful and most wonderful have been, and are being, evolved.

Reflecting on his long career and his influence on the wider scientific community, Darwin wrote in 1876:

> My success as a man of science, whatever this may have amounted to, has been determined, as far as I can judge, by complex and diversified mental qualities and conditions. Of these the most important have been-the love of science-unbounded patience in long reflecting over any subject-industry in observing and collecting facts-and a fair share of invention as well as common sense. With such abilities as I possess, it is truly surprising that thus I should have influenced to a considerable extent the beliefs of scientific men on some important points.

The marriage of Charles and Emma was a love match and when the end came, it was their abiding wish that the two should lie beside each other in the tiny cemetery of the village church at Downe. But on his death in 1882 at the age of seventy-three, such was the love and respect for Darwin and his achievements amongst his academic colleagues and the public at large that his final resting place was to be Westminster Abbey. Among the pall-bearers was Alfred Russel Wallace, the man who had shocked Darwin in 1858 by presenting him with a sketch so similar to the idea that he had wrestled with for decades and forced him reluctantly into print. Wallace had spent the intervening years in the shadow of Darwin and in the years since has too often been omitted from the story. His conclusions on the origin of species are closely entwined with Darwin's but it seems history only has room for one icon at a time. It is as much a measure of Wallace's character as it is of his respect for Darwin, the elder statesman of science, that he played so poignant a role in the funeral ceremony.

There is so much of Shrewsbury in Darwin and so much of Darwin in Shrewsbury and because of this, the town is so much more than simply his

The unveiling of Darwin's statue outside the town library, 10 August 1894.

birthplace. Is it possible to define precisely why Shrewsbury made such a difference in Darwin's life and career? Perhaps this book has gone some way towards that end and one day you may travel to Shrewsbury to see the sights that Darwin saw and perhaps draw your own conclusions. When you do visit and stand beside the Darwin Gate, don't forget to take a few steps down Mardol and look back at the three pillars where all Darwin's influences combine to create one unifying image that symbolises his great idea, the origin of species.

The Darwin Walk

The Darwin Walk was devised by the author in 2003. The route is largely contained within the loop of the River Severn and at a steady pace should take no more than an hour. However, Shrewsbury is very attractive and there are many distractions, not least several excellent cafes, restaurants, and traditional English pubs. Also, it is a good idea to look up now and again for even the most ordinary of shopfronts may sit beneath medieval timber frames or boast ornate carvings that are well worth pausing to admire. Strolling the streets of Shrewsbury is like taking a trip through time. Don't be afraid to explore the alleys or shuts and passages as you make your way to the next point on the walk. And if the weather is clement, a stroll to the beautiful Dingle in the Quarry Park won't disappoint anyone who enjoys a good floral display. So, let's begin the Darwin Walk. Use the map at the end of this book as your guide.

The Bellstone

Across the road from Shrewsbury's twentieth-century Market Hall are two wrought-iron gates that lead you through an archway to a small, paved courtyard. At the end of the courtyard, a set of steps lead up to the Morris Hall, a prime example of Arts & Crafts design. At the foot of the steps rests a large boulder known locally as The Bellstone; this rock has travelled far.

Shropshire may boast a treasury of stone in its landscape but The Bellstone is not from these parts; it is what locals might refer to as an in-comer. This stone originates from the county of Cumbria or possibly even the Scottish Borders. In Darwin's childhood, The Bellstone was a puzzle. Who would transport a stone so far and for no apparent purpose?

In his biography, Darwin remembers a local amateur naturalist, a Mr Cotton, saying to the young boy, 'The world will come to an end before we learn how this stone came to rest here.'

Some years later, at Edinburgh, Darwin was learning about the action of the glaciers during the last ice age; how the land was carved and brutally scarred by the sheer force and weight of the ice and how boulders far greater than The Bellstone were nudged across the earth's surface only to be stranded when the ice receded and later, to become known as erratics. In that instant and with that revelation, he recalled the words of Mr Cotton and 'marvelled at the progress of science'.

The entrance to the Morris Hall courtyard, scene of the annual Darwin Birthday Toast and location of the Bellstone.

The Bellstone.

Darwin learned that things do not have to remain a mystery if we have the curiosity to ask questions. It is this simple anecdote that made the courtyard the ideal location for an annual toast to Darwin at noon on his birthday, 12th February.

13 Claremont*

Around the corner from the Morris Hall yard and The Bellstone is a narrow, flag-stoned road called Claremont. The short road leads from the town centre to the entrance to the town park known as The Quarry. Halfway up the street on the left-hand side is No. 13. This was the home of the Revd George Case, a minister at the Unitarian Church which Darwin attended with his mother. It was here that Darwin received his first formal education. He remembers little of his time here but does recall one incident which occurred behind the house in the churchyard of St Chad's. One day, Darwin was looking from a rear window and saw the spectacle of the burial of a dragoon officer. It's perhaps worth noting that Darwin was born during a time of turmoil and great uncertainty. Darwin was born four

---

*This is a private residence, please do not disturb the owners.

13 Claremont, former home of Revd George Case.

years after the Battle of Trafalgar and six years before the Battle of Waterloo. Throughout his early years, Europe was embroiled in conflict and the threat of invasion was ever-present.

In that age, one dressed for battle as well as for dinner, with bright tunics adorned with gold braid, gleaming sabres and tall hats festooned with feathers. Darwin recalls, 'How clearly I can still see the horse with the man's empty boots and carbine suspended from the saddle. And the firing over the grave. This scene deeply stirred whatever poetic fancy there was in me.'

St Chad's Church

Continue to the top of the street and turn left. Here you will find St Chad's Church, an impressive building that overlooks the town and the Quarry Park where grassy slopes roll down to the banks of the river. It was here that Charles Darwin was baptised.

The main body of the church is circular in shape and well worth a look inside. The present baptismal font is fashioned from limestone and closer inspection reveals a myriad of marine fossils, set like jewels in its form.

Knowing what we do about the family's beliefs, it does beg the question why was a Unitarian baptised in an Anglican church? In the early part of the nineteenth century, nonconformists were still barred from some sections of society such as public office

St Chad's Church.

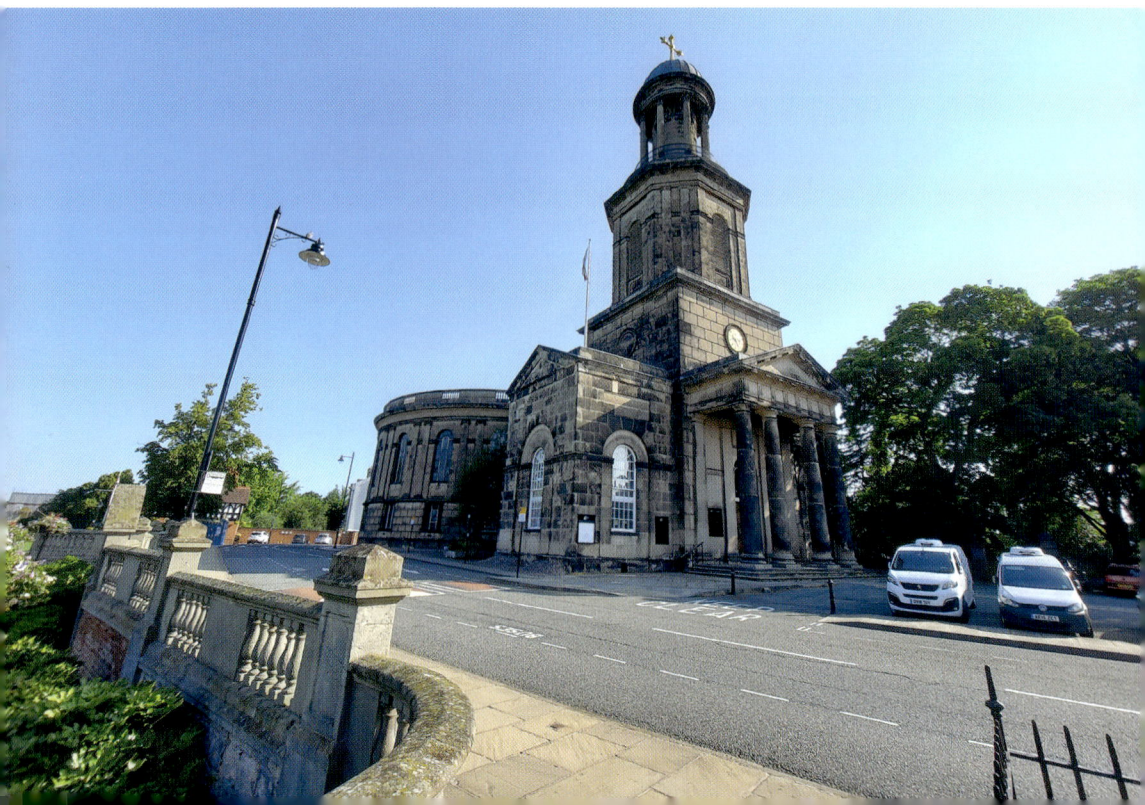

and obtaining degrees at universities like Oxford and Cambridge. Perhaps Robert was playing the long game and ensuring his son could access higher education.

It was also the case that Darwin's mother, Susannah, was more closely associated with the Unitarian movement than Robert. So, the answer may be simpler. St Chad's was and is the church where civic services are conducted and Robert, as a pillar of the community, would have had some association with the church. A family christening would reflect the family's position in Shrewsbury society.

The Unitarian Church

Shrewsbury did not entirely escape the planning faux pas of the late twentieth century, but has mercifully retained much of its historic integrity. The High Street is a case in point. Narrow and bustling, it would be easy to rush by and miss the Unitarian Church, squeezed as it is between a row of shops. Best viewed from across the street, the Italianate, stone facade dates from 1885. The original building was erected in 1689 and enlarged in 1709.

The Unitarian Church.

Its chequered history includes an act of arson by a Jacobean mob in 1715 which gutted the building, though it was soon rebuilt. The church is still a place of worship for Shrewsbury's Unitarians and is used as a venue during the annual Darwin Festival. Inside is a plaque to mark the fact that Darwin worshipped here with his mother and one that notes the poet Samuel Taylor Coleridge once preached from its pulpit. A plaque outlining the Unitarian Path is attached to the front of the church to the right of the doors. It distils the ethos that allowed Darwin to think freely and question the received wisdom of the day.

The Lion Hotel

At a time when a coach and horses were the fastest way to travel, coaching inns were important refuelling stations and played a vital part in the logistics of the country's transport network. Shrewsbury is on the A5, a key route that links London to Holyhead and then, by ferry, to Ireland. Pre-telegraph, this coach road would have been a vital conduit between the seat of the British government and its interests across the Irish Sea.

The Lion Hotel was Shrewsbury's premier coaching inn. It stands at the top of Wyle Cop, a steep, picturesque shopping street that looks out beyond the confines

The Lion Hotel.

of town to open countryside and the Wrekin Hill a few miles away. Though wider than most streets in Shrewsbury, Wyle Cop is narrow by comparison to roads in other towns. The arch that leads from the street to the stable yard behind the hotel is also narrow and barely wide enough for a coach to pass through. Yet one coachman, through his skill and bravado, turned the arrival of the London to Holyhead coach into a spectacle for townsfolk. Sam Hayward would urge his team of horses up the slope at full tilt, swing the team and coach round a 45-degree angle and plunge through the narrow entrance with only inches to spare on either side to gasps of amazement from onlookers and a round of enthusiastic applause.

Imagine if you will, the mailbags being loaded and amongst the letters, one from Darwin to Francis Beaufort pleading to be reconsidered for the position of naturalist on HMS *Beagle* having previously turned down the offer owing to his father's initial objections. Imagine, sometime later, a young Charles Darwin climbing into the coach to begin the journey south having secured the position after finally being granted permission by his father to set sail on the voyage of a lifetime. This is where his great adventure began.

The Library

Shrewsbury's main library is an imposing building. Facing Shrewsbury Castle, the two act as a gateway from the north and stand a few hundred yards from the narrow slip of land that attaches the town to the wider landscape, Shrewsbury being almost completely encircled by a loop of the River Severn.

Shrewsbury Library.

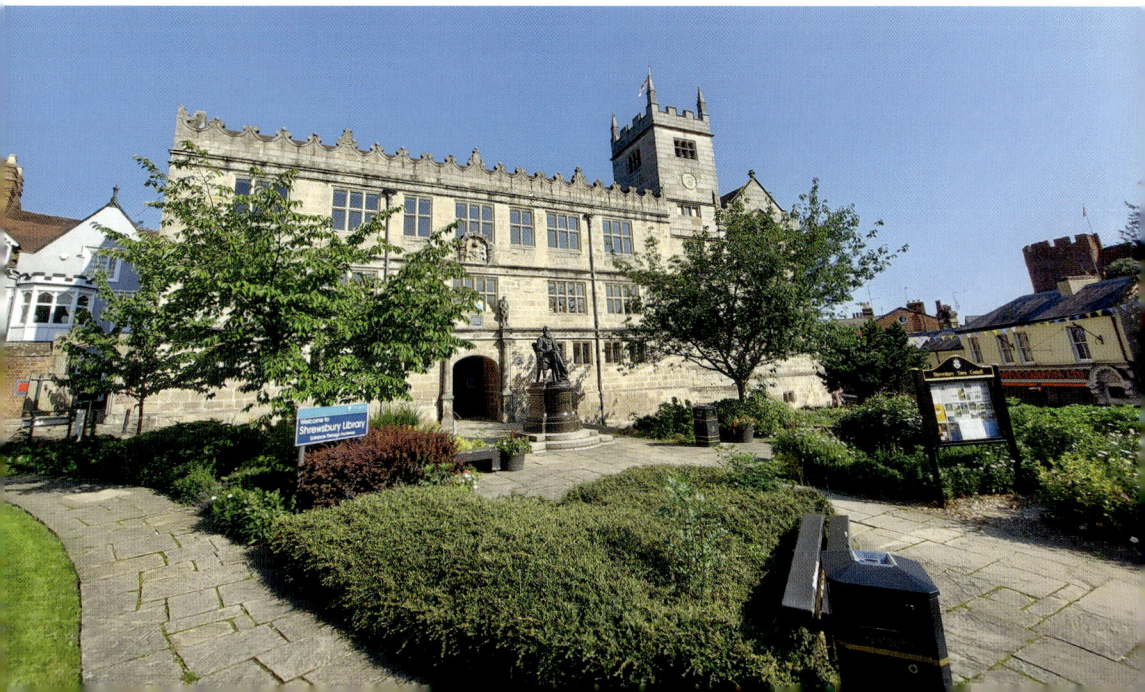

In a previous life, the library was Shrewsbury School. The Music Room on the top floor still retains the high, vaulted ceilings and the oak wood panelling displays the initials of bored pupils engraved with their penknives during endless lectures in Greek or Latin.

Outside the library is a statue of Shrewsbury's most famous son, unveiled in 1897. Reflecting on his unhappy memories of his time here, it is perhaps apt that he has been modelled seated with his back to the school. His recollections are less about Dr Butler's lessons and more of his stolen moments at home before dashing back across the river before lights out. The classics were not to his liking and even by the age of eight when he arrived here, Darwin had developed a fascination with the natural world, a world not contained in the textbooks at Shrewsbury School.

The Darwin Gate

Here at the head of a street called Mardol stands a piece of public art called the Darwin Gate. The three key influences or pillars that provided Darwin with the foundations of a life in science are here made real.

The Darwin Gate.

Standing alongside the structure, imagine if you will that they represent in turn the rich geological landscape of Shropshire, the Unitarian Path and the Darwin family garden diaries; here are the solid representations of those three pillars. It is possible to stand beside the Darwin Gate in such a way that one of the three pillars is obscured from view. In that position, one could argue to passers-by that the piece consists of only two pillars and not three. One could choose to remain there and continue to argue for all time that there are only two pillars and not three or one could choose to move to one side where two pillars become three. It's all about perspective.

Darwin was not necessarily the first to see the things he observed on the voyage but he was perhaps the first to see them with the perspective his upbringing had afforded him. In effect, he shifted his view and saw a bigger picture – in the same way that the Darwin Gate appears to change if one walks a short distance down Mardol and looks back at the structure. From this new position, the disparate finials appear to come together as one unified form just as Darwin himself drew together disparate facts and observations to create a single, unifying idea that explained the diversity of life on Earth.

Quantum Leap

In 2009, institutions across the world celebrated the dual anniversaries of Darwin's 200th birthday and the 150th anniversary of the publication of his great work *On the Origin of Species*.

Shrewsbury, as his birthplace, was at the heart of those celebrations. In Darwin's home town, the arts and sciences combined in a burst of creativity which produced not only a series of lectures but dance, music and drama commissions, festivals, and school projects.

The town already boasted two pieces of public art with connections to the great man: his statue outside the library and the Darwin Gate. Alongside the celebrations, the town wanted a more permanent reminder of the anniversary year and set about commissioning a new piece of public art to be sited on the riverbank in a small park close to the Welsh Bridge.

The commission was awarded to Pearce & Lal who proposed an audacious structure that would stretch the limits of engineering but ultimately result in an installation that combines mechanical ingenuity with organic patterns. At 12 meters high and 17.5 metres long, the structure is comprised of several identical propeller-shaped, concrete lozenges stacked in such a way that each piece is rotated slightly away from the one before. The effect is that the piece appears to rotate or twist, whilst describing an arch.

On the ground below the arch, a narrow line of tiles snakes across the ground in a pattern that reflects the loop of the River Severn and along this line the

Quantum Leap.

story of the earth is laid out, from the Big Bang to the arrival of Mankind. It's sobering to note how late our arrival is in the great span of time and consider the disproportionate impact we have made.

The Mount

In its early history, because of the embrace of the River Severn, Shrewsbury was only accessible from the north by foot from the area now known as Castlefields. Elsewhere fords were the only way to cross and gain access to the market town. It's why Roger de Montgomery chose Shrewsbury for his base and not the nearby site

The Mount.

of the Roman city of Viroconium, building his Norman fortification overlooking the narrow land bridge. Fords were eventually replaced by bridges and two in particular reflect the border nature of the town: to the east, English Bridge and to the west, the Welsh Bridge. A short walk from Quantum Leap across the Welsh Bridge brings the traveller to the area of town known as Frankwell. It was here, as the road to Wales rises slowly away from the town, that Robert Darwin elected to build the family home. Close to the gate at the end of the drive is a plaque explaining Darwin's connection with the property. Through the gate, the drive winds gently towards the coach yard and outbuildings where Ras and Charles 'Gas' Darwin undertook their chemistry experiments. It's here that you get a glimpse of the impressive frontage of the house and the portico entrance where the young Darwin expressed the desire 'to know something about every pebble in front of the hall door'. Continued on page 96.

The Mount

Doctor's Field

Mount House ■

COPTHORNE ROAD

NEW STREET

FRANKWELL

Frankwell

Copthorne

■ **Theatre Severn**

Welsh Bridge

Quantum Leap ■

SMITHFIELD

CLAREMONT BANK

BARKER ST

Porthill
Footbridge

The Quarry
Park

13 Claremont ■

■ **The Belst**

St Chad's
Church

Old Mark

The Dingle

TOWN WALLS

NORTH

Kingsland
Toll Bridge

*Shrewsbury
School*

RIV

Kingsland

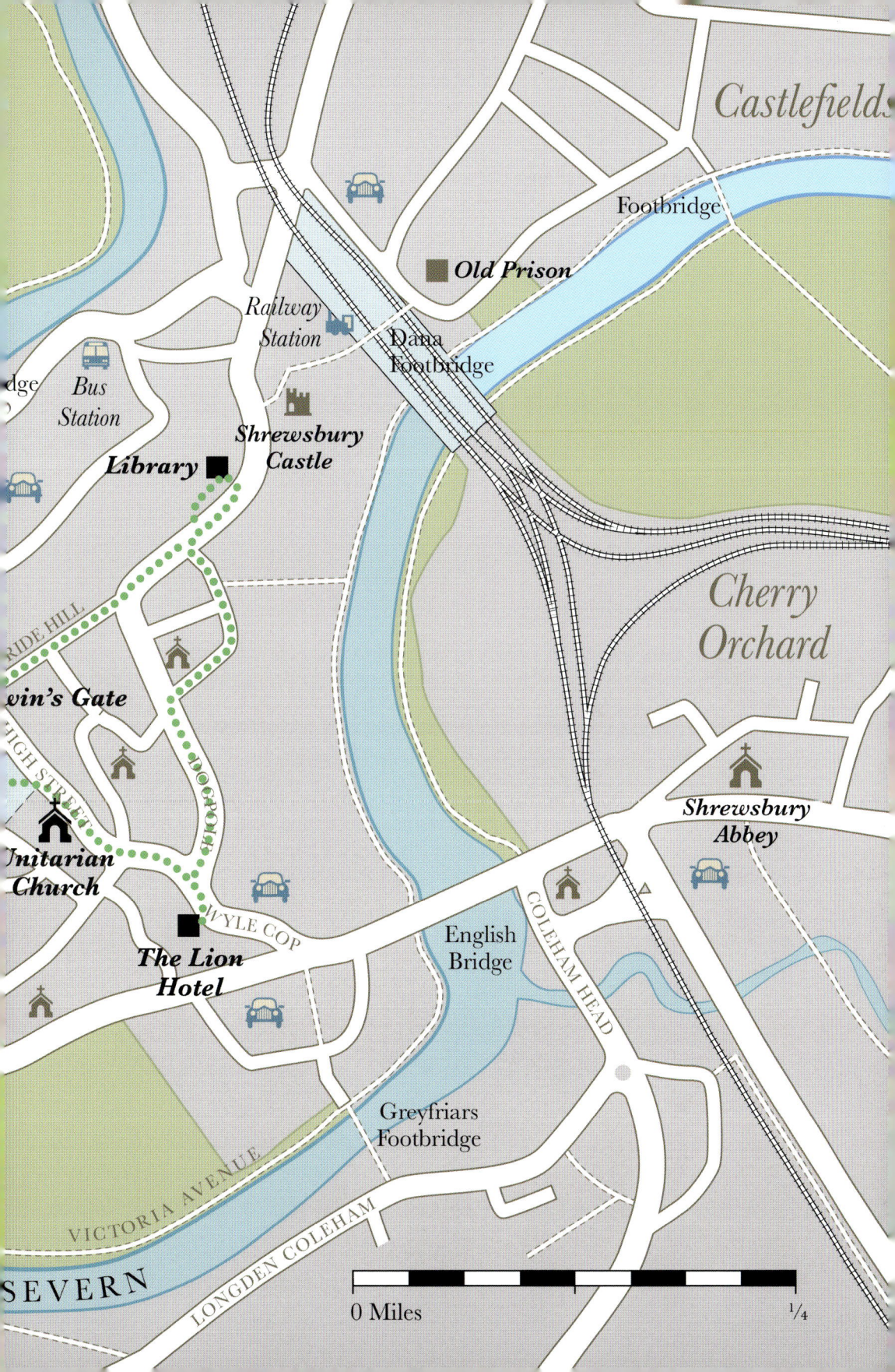

Castlefields

🚗

■ **Old Prison**

Footbridge

Railway
Station

🚉

Dana
Footbridge

🚌 **Bus**
Station

dge

🏰

🚗

Library ■

Shrewsbury
Castle

⛪

Cherry
Orchard

RIDE HILL

vin's Gate

⛪

HIGH STREET

DOGPOLE

⛪

⛪ **Shrewsbury**
Abbey

🚗

Unitarian
Church

⛪

■

WYLE COP

🚗

COLEHAM HEAD

△

The Lion
Hotel

English
Bridge

⛪

🚗

Greyfriars
Footbridge

VICTORIA AVENUE

LONGDEN COLEHAM

SEVERN

0 Miles

¼

To the west beyond the current boundary fence, one looks down Darwin Gardens, the street named after and built on the gardens tended so dutifully by the Darwin family and recorded so fastidiously in their perennial garden diaries.

Seven years after the publication of *Origin*, family ties with The Mount were finally severed. Darwin's sister Susan never married and lived in the family house until her death at the age of sixty-three in 1866. In November of that year, a six-day sale of the house and contents took place. Among the lots were mundane items: Lot 31, three brushes and a mop; and Lot 45, a quantity of perforated zinc. But alongside the mundane were items that reflected the family's love of horticulture: Lot 10, nine large orange trees in pots; Lot 11, a quantity of Azaleas; and Lot 12, a quantity of camellias. This truly was the end of an era. This was the house from which the schoolboy Darwin ran to reach his dormitory at Shrewsbury School before the bell tolled for the end of the day. This was the house which Darwin and his mother, Susannah, left to attend services at the Unitarian Church and this was the house from which Darwin set off for study at Edinburgh and Cambridge universities. From here his exploration of the wider landscape sparked his interest in the natural sciences. From here he would set off for Maer for sublime summer evenings with his Uncle Jos and from here he travelled to Woodhouse to meet with his girlfriend, Fanny Owen. It was from here that he set off south to join the *Beagle* and it was to here that he returned after the journey of a lifetime. It was from here that the bachelor set off for St Peter's Church, Maer, to marry his beloved Emma but above all, this is the house where Charles Darwin was born, an inquisitive child with a lively imagination beginning a remarkable journey of discovery and Shrewsbury is where the mind was made.

Plan your trip to Darwin's Shrewsbury now at visitshropshire.co.uk